Canadian Pacific Railway Stations in British Columbia

Ian Baird

ORCA BOOK PUBLISHERS

Copyright © 1990 by Ian Baird

All rights reserved. No part of this book may be reproduced without the written permission of the publisher, except by a reviewer, who may quote passages in a review.

Canadian Cataloguing in Publication Data
Baird, Ian, 1947-
   Canadian Pacific Railway stations in B.C.

   ISBN 0-920501-52-4
   1. Railroads — British Columbia — Stations — History. 2. Canadian Pacific Railway Company — History. 3. CP Rail — History. I. Title
   TF302.B7B34 1990   385'.314'09711   C90-091483-1

Orca Book Publishers Ltd.
P.O. Box 5626, Stn. B,
Victoria, B.C., V8R 6S4

Cover design by Rick Dykun
Typeset by the University of Victoria Students' Society Graphics Shop
Printed in Canada
Front cover photo: Mt. Stephen House, Field, B.C.
Back cover photos: (l to r) Lakeshore station, Sicamous, Brilliant, Roger's Pass

To Arthur (Robbie) Robinson, who served on the Esquimalt and Nanaimo Railway mail service from 1916 to September 30, 1952.

Acknowledgments

I am deeply indebted to the following individuals for their advice, encouragement, loan of photographs and an understanding of my long and ongoing obsession with railway stations: Howard Gerwing, John Hoffmeister, Don MacLachan, Chris Main, Archie Millar, Chris Petter, Penny Seedhouse and Elwood White.

Appreciation is also extended to the following organizations for their assistance: British Columbia Archives and Research Service, British Columbia Railway Historical Society, Canadian Pacific Corporate Archives, Vancouver Public Library and the Victoria City Archives.

Special mention must be extended to the following individuals: Dave Wilkie, who gave many hours of advice that only someone of his experience can offer, and to Dr. Alan Gowans, who was my professor in Art History at the University of Victoria and gave the initial stimulus and encouragement to this project. A special thank you to Trudy Byers, who typed the manuscript and put up with my many additions and deletions, and finally, Martin Segger, who painstakingly edited the manuscript and captions many times. I may have missed some people, and to those, my sincere apologies.

Contents

Stations in B.C. map	6
Foreword	9
Introduction	11
Chapter One: A History of the CPR in B.C.	13
Vancouver Island and the E & N Railway	13
British Columbia and the CPR	14
Chapter Two: Architectural Features of CPR Railway Stations	17
Chapter Three: Railway Stations by Division	20
Part One: Vancouver Island	20
Part Two: Vancouver	32
Part Three: Kettle Valley	48
Part Four: Kootenay	63
Part Five: Revelstoke	83
Bibliography	103
Notes	105
Index	107

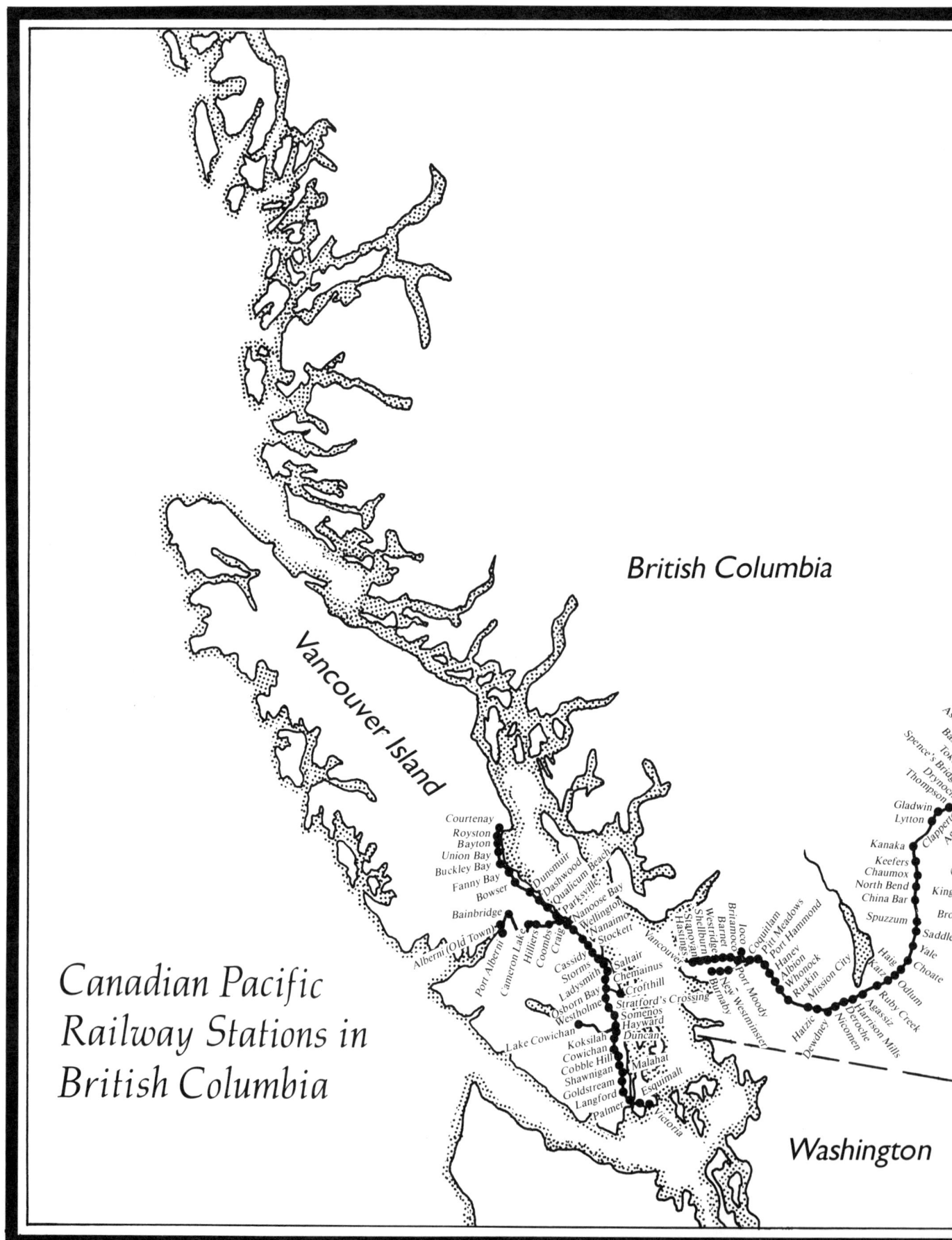

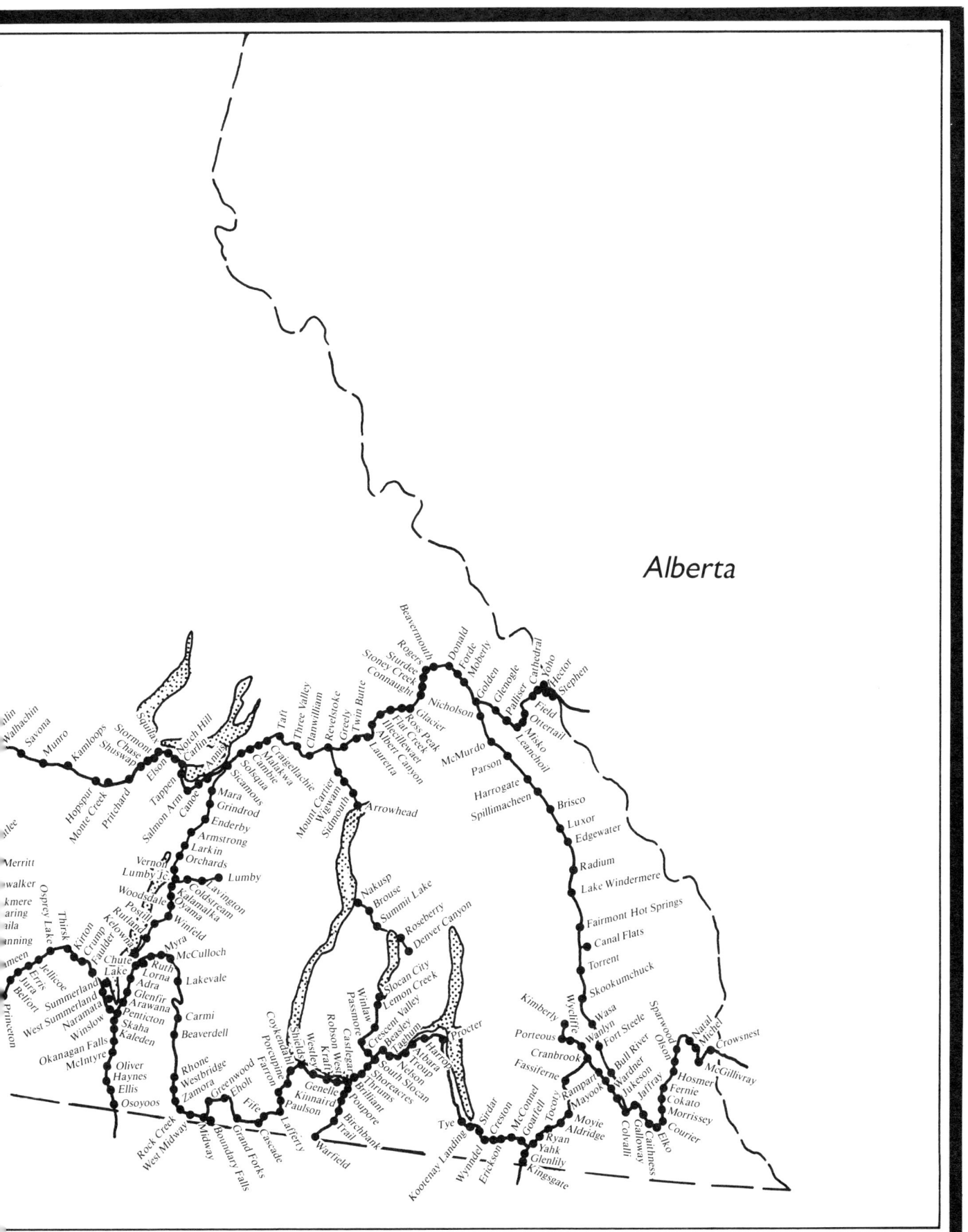

Foreword

Like most immigrants to Canada pre-1960, my introduction was by rail. Mother, father and three boys flew into Winnipeg on a much-overworked DC 8. Dad had booked us rail passage to the station nearest his Saskatchewan teaching post. We boarded the gleaming aluminum-and-steel Canadian in the early hours of the morning and headed west. The stateroom was luxurious, and we all put our shoes in the locker so marked. Yes, magically they had been cleaned and buffed the next morning. We three boys claimed seats in the dome car and settled into the leather, tapestry and plastic pastel decor to watch twilit Canada come alive as we sped through the wide-screen prairie landscape. Everything was twice life-size, particularly the trains.

In Swift Current we transferred to the local milk run: a heavy-breathing steam freight. We were the only passengers on the last car, a holdover from the Wild West. As we shunted, groaned and creaked down the line, picking up grain cars at every stop, we all inhaled the hot, dusty air which had over years impregnated the horsehair seats. Smoke and grit seeped through the rattling windows. The pot-belly stove with its gun-metal gleam smelled of stale ashes; or was it the cinders from the panting engine way ahead? Lunch provided our introduction to the small prairie station. Dull reddish-brown, blistered by years of dusty heat, chinook winds and blizzard snows, the small, squat building championed the name "Lancer" on a fading white-and-black signboard fixed to the clapboard wall. The brakeman said they would blow the whistle when they were ready to go, and to come by the engine so they would know we were back on board. Debbie Reynolds sang "Tammy" on the cafe jukebox as we all ate our first real Saskatchewan porkchops-and-panfries lunch off thick Medalta dinnerware. We then lumbered on to Leader where we got off to make the last few miles to Burstall by car.

Burstall, another typical prairie small town, and home to us for two years, was blessed with only a bi-weekly freight. We lived in the shadows of a sentinel row of elevators, and the station provided a focal point for Main Street, which mercifully terminated in a moat-like swamp that separated affairs of the line from those of the dusty gridiron town. The CPR agent was a crusty man who ranked with the elevator manager, the pool-hall operator and a part-time United Church parson as civic luminaries. Hundreds of Canadian towns were the same in 1957, and had been since the turn of the century. Innocent then, I now know I was privileged to have caught the end of an era and a way of life.

Later, there were numerous other trips on the Canadian, from Vancouver to an Edmonton boarding school. Dome-car views of the Rockies at night, where moonlight ricocheted off the snowclad mountainsides, created a vast luminescent corridor into which the molten shadow edges of the forests intruded. One could feel the subzero crispness of the winter night as the steel wheels bit the icy rail. To a sixteen-year-old, it was an honour to be offered a "snort" from the whisky flask of a travelling salesman: "Been doin' it since '35," his only comment in a gravelly, midwestern accent. What exactly he had "been doin'" has pricked my imagination ever since.

Of the time when rail lines were laid at the rate of a mile a day and stations thrown up to match, Ian Baird writes, "These were the boom years, and the CPR boomed with them." He also sadly laments towns such as Natal and Michel, "now gone except for the railway station at Natal and hotel at the latter . . ."

This book is timely. As the last stations disappear, it is important to remember these early urban symbols that with great pretence defined the British Columbia settlement landscape. Sometimes appropriately academic, but also evocative, this text and its accompanying photographs relive the creation years of the railway era. The stations were a crucible for British Columbia's urban history. They were what temples were to classical Greece, forums were to imperial Rome, churches to medieval Europe. However, unlike those precedents, they were flimsy wooden structures, technology-dependent on the fortunes of a fast-changing industrial world. Their passage needs to be marked, and Ian Baird eloquently does so here.

Martin Segger
Victoria, 1990

Introduction

In the forging of the Canadian nation, one of the greatest accomplishments was the securing of a railway from sea to sea. This railway, the Canadian Pacific, was one of the conditions of British Columbia's entry into the Canadian Confederation.

Prior to completion of the line, the fledgling colony of British Columbia did more trade south of the United States border than east of the Rockies. The Crown Colony of British Columbia was the result of the union of the colonies of Vancouver Island and British Columbia in 1866. With the exception of the small province of Manitoba, which had entered the Canadian union on July 15, 1870, the immense area between Ontario and the Rockies was basically an uninhabited wilderness. Formerly the fiefdom of the Hudson's Bay Company, this land was acquired from the Company in 1867 and was called the Northwest Territories. In 1905 the provinces of Alberta and Saskatchewan were formed, and the boundaries of Manitoba were enlarged in 1881, 1884 and 1912 to the extent they are today.

While annexation organizations made repeated demands for subsuming Canada into the U.S.A., Sir John A. MacDonald had seen the threat of the Fenian Raids and knew that if a railway was not built, the territories may very well fall into the American orbit. The CPR had a difficult beginning, but it did accomplish its task, and ahead of schedule. We often extol the accomplishments of the directors of the syndicate, but in many a nameless grave across the face of our nation lay the remains of the navvies who laboured sixteen hours a day for what now seems to be a pittance. The average wage was $3 a day, with $4 deducted per week for room and board.

Once the railway was completed, the infrastructure required to support it was enormous. In this book I pay tribute to the station agents, who, often on duty twenty-four hours a day, were responsible for the day-to-day operation of their stations, the nerve centres of their community. Now only a memory, these station agents were a vital force in knitting this country together.

When driving through today's extensive British Columbia highway system, we may occasionally find an abandoned station in general decay with its signal posts removed. If it could speak, what stories it could tell.

Chapter One: A History of the CPR in British Columbia

Vancouver Island received its railway as a part of the conditions for British Columbia's entry into Confederation in 1871. The line was not started until July 1873, when Prime Minister John A. Macdonald felt that "he must take some action to demonstrate minimal progress on the railroad."[1] Thus the decision to start the railway at Esquimalt on July 19, 1873.

From 1873 until 1883, Vancouver Island suffered through a severe economic depression. A major cause of this depression was the method of financing the new railway. A grant to the federal government put a reserve on all unsettled lands for twenty miles on either side of the proposed line. The population north of Victoria felt isolated, as the only contact with the capital was by steamer. Prospective settlers were unable to purchase land along the railway belt due to the federal grant, and this resulted in economic stagnation. To worsen matters further, the provincial government in Victoria would not move to help finance a road from Victoria north as it maintained that the road would be redundant once the railway was completed.

A further delay to the railway was caused by the defeat of the Macdonald government in 1873. The Liberals succeeded to office under Alexander Mackenzie. They possessed no coherent railway policy, and discussions floundered. Hence, Premier Walkem of British Columbia decided to approach the Imperial government, "for settlement of extra-provincial questions was still strong in all provincial capitals, for the Dominion was less than seven years old."[2] Lord Carnarvon, then Colonial Secretary, readily offered his services as an arbitrator. After deliberation, Lord Carnarvon agreed that a line should be built. Lord Dufferin, the Governor General, observed the dispute with concern and suggested that he visit British Columbia in an attempt to resolve the issue. Indeed, he did visit Victoria in August of 1876. It was a triumphal welcoming, with the fanfare typical of those days. He supported the Carnarvon terms of 1874, which stipulated that a railway should be built, but he would have no talk of secession if it was not built.

Lord Dufferin obviously felt Vancouver Islanders had been slighted by the Mackenzie government. He delivered a conciliatory speech in Victoria on September 14, 1876, which went a long way to quell the fires of secession. However, his promises all came to naught, and the railway issue climaxed when Vancouver Islanders sent a secession petition to Queen Victoria which was intercepted by the Governor General. It is interesting to speculate on what would have happened had the Queen received it.

In the general election of 1878, the Mackenzie government was defeated. However, as the Conservative leader Macdonald was defeated in his Kingston, Ontario, riding, he accepted the invitation to stand as Victoria's Member of Parliament and was duly elected. The Tories moved at once on the railway issue by announcing on May 3, 1879, a promise to build one hundred miles of railway in British Columbia. No firm decision had been reached with regard to the Vancouver Island section, and the ugly spectre of separation was raised again by Premier Walkem.

Negotiations dragged on until "in 1883, William Smithe, Cowichan's Member of the Legislative Assembly, became Premier of the Province of British Columbia, at which time he quickly cleared the way for

13

construction of the Esquimalt and Nanaimo Railway. His peace party pushed through the Settlement Act of 1883, which the previous administration, led by Premier Walkem, had obstructed."[3] Smithe was very interested in the railway issue because his riding was on Vancouver Island. He had won the electoral district of Cowichan in the general election of July 24, 1882, with 102 votes out of 143 cast, a 71.33 per cent approval rating.

The result of this election was that the caretaker administration of Robert Beaven was out of office. However, in those days you had to stand for re-election before taking a cabinet post. Accordingly, a writ was issued on January 29, 1883, with nomination day being the following 15th of February. By acclamation, Smithe took his seat as member and Premier of the province on February 19, 1883.

George Walkem, the premier before Beaven, had represented Cariboo in the legislature, and many Vancouver Islanders felt that because of his mainland attachments he had not pushed the Island cause with enough vigour. Ironically, many on the mainland felt that with the election of the Smithe government, Vancouver Island was being singled out for special treatment.

In December 1883, the restriction on the grant was lifted, and the land was made available for settlement at a rate of $1 per acre for a four-year period.

The common perception is that the contract for construction of the Esquimalt and Nanaimo Railway was first awarded to the Dunsmuir Syndicate. However, this is not the case. As Donald MacLachan tells us in his book *The Esquimalt & Nanaimo Railway — The Dunsmuir Years: 1884-1905*, the contract was initially awarded to an American firm, the Vancouver Land and Railway Company, headed by L.M. Clement of San Francisco.

In the end, the company was unable to provide the necessary financial security, so the deal collapsed. Sir John A. Macdonald stepped into the act. He was able to persuade Robert Dunsmuir to take on the project. Dunsmuir then formed a syndicate comprised of himself and some of his associates at the Central Pacific Railroad in California. They were J. Bryden, Charles Crocker, C.F. Crocker, C.P. Huntingdon, Leland Stanford and James Dunsmuir. Out of the 15,000 shares issued, Robert Dunsmuir held 7,450. Construction proceeded quickly, with the first stake to mark the southern terminus being driven on May 7, 1884. To Prime Minister Sir John A. Macdonald went the honour of driving the last spike at Cliffside near Shawnigan Lake on August 13, 1886.

Dunsmuir was very pleased with the progress and accordingly extended the line to Esquimalt on September 24, 1886, with a further extension in 1887 to Wellington, 4.8 miles north of Nanaimo. There he established a roundhouse and workshop, and this was to remain the headquarters of the E & N until 1913, when the shops were relocated to Victoria. The need to extend the line to downtown Victoria became readily apparent, and on March 8, 1888, the first train arrived in the city. The Victoria terminal consisted of a station with freight sheds and the CPR offices, which were quartered in the adjacent Janion Hotel (where they remained until 1944). Only the Janion building remains. This was the Esquimalt and Nanaimo Railway until 1905, when the CPR acquired the line.

British Columbia and the Canadian Pacific Railway

When British Columbia joined Confederation in 1871, the terms of union promised a railway that was to be constructed within ten years. Sir Sandford Fleming undertook a series of surveys commencing in 1871-1872. His work located "the line to the north of Lake Superior, across the northern prairies and through the Yellowhead Pass down to tidewater on the Pacific."[4] During these years, the majority of the population in the new province of British Columbia lived in or near Victoria. As a result, agitation grew in favour of a route down Bute Inlet, across Seymour Narrows and eventually down to Victoria. However, as events turned out, the Rogers Pass route, named after the redoubtable engineer, was chosen. Rogers was a thorough eccentric, yet he was frightfully competent. It is said that Rogers never cashed the cheque issued to him by the CPR for discovering the pass, preferring to keep it as a souvenir.

After what must have seemed an eternity to residents of British Columbia, who threatened secession due to lack of progress on the railway, CPR steel finally crossed the B.C. border on May 25, 1884. Appropriately enough, the first station on the line within B.C. was named Stephen, after the first president of the CPR. Many difficulties had plagued this far-flung arm of the transcontinental railway.

Following the terms of union and the Fleming surveys, the contract for construction of the railway was awarded to Sir Hugh Allan, president of the Allan steamship line and a staunch supporter of Macdonald and the Tory party. All seemed well until the Pacific Scandal of 1873, when it was revealed that Sir Hugh had made substantial contributions to the Tories' election coffers. The end result was the resignation of Macdonald's government on November 5, 1983, and the formation of a ministry under Grit leader Alexander Mackenzie. Mackenzie's administration was returned in the general election of 1874.

A dour Scot, Mackenzie did not believe in the economic justification for the railway, so he vacillated and compromised by pursuing a lake and rail approach. That is to say, a railway to one end of Lake Superior, then by steamer, then rail at the other end. Fortunately for Canada, and foremost for the future of the railway, his government was defeated in 1878, and Macdonald's railway policy, albeit in an altered form, carried on. The revamped terms of construction, agreed upon by Parliament on February 15, 1881, provided for a syndicate known as the Canadian Pacific Railway to execute this gargantuan task.

Due to the mountainous nature of B.C., construction difficulties were onerous. One section, that from Yale to Kamloops, was under contract by the government to Andrew Onderdonk, an American engineer. This section was 127 miles long, and the difficulties encountered here were comparable to those encountered on the Lake Superior section. Another difficult section was the line between Hector and Field, a distance of 4.4 miles in which the grade descended 1,141 feet, exceeding the line's specifications of a 4 per cent grade. Runaway tracks were provided in the event of mechanical failure, and Van Horne was quick to explain that this situation was only temporary.

Snow proved a major problem; indeed, avalanches sometimes reached speeds of 200 miles per hour. To help alleviate this problem, Ross, the chief engineer for this section, "built the line beyond Rogers Pass to avoid the avalanche slopes and steep grades, using a series of trestles to create 'The Loop.'"[5] With collective drive and energy, the railway was completed, and the last spike was driven at Craigellachie in the Eagle Pass on November 7, 1885.

For a description of the completed route in British Columbia, let us turn to the noted historian Alexander Begg, who described the route through the Rockies in a paper entitled *Canada and Its National Highway*, which was read before the Society of Arts in London, England, on March 23, 1886:

"Leaving Laggan, we pass under the shadow of the mountain, and cross wild mountain streams, and shortly stop at Stephen, named after the President of the Canadian Pacific Railway, to whom the successful prosecution of the enterprise is so largely due. This is the highest elevation on the railway, the road being 5,300 feet above the sea. Westward from Stephen, the track passes several mountain lakes, from one of which several streams flow on one side to the Atlantic, and on the other side to the nearest waters of the Pacific. Five miles beyond is Kicking Horse Lake, whence the Kicking Horse River empties into the Columbia. The track proceeds down the Kicking Horse Valley amid scenery more magnificent than ever before, to the north bank of the Beaver River, and spans the Columbia River, thence crossing the Selkirk Range by Rogers Pass, named after its discoverer, Major Rogers, an approximate distance from Stephen of 100 miles. The railway now continues for forty miles through a valley to the second crossing of the Columbia River. The line then passes through the Eagle Pass, and on through the valley of the Thompson River to Kamloops. Continuing through the valley and coasting Kamloops Lake, the track reaches Savona Ferry. Still keeping to the basin of the Thompson, and following the gorge through which the river forces its way, the railway leaves the westerly direction it has hitherto pursued and bends down to the south. Crossing the Nicola River, we reach Lytton, near where the Thompson River enters the parent water of the Fraser. Crossing the Fraser, the line proceeds on the western bank past Yale to Hope, where a westerly course is again resumed to Vancouver, the Pacific terminus of the Canadian Pacific Railway."[6]

The force of the personalities which caused this

transportation miracle was remarkable. Cornelius Van Horne (1843-1915) was a man of extreme energy and discipline. Van Horne was American by birth and rose to become manager of the Canadian Pacific Railway. He seemed destined for a railroad career — his first job was as a timekeeper for the Illinois Central Railroad. His energy knew no bounds. Van Horne believed in working hard and playing hard. One story relates that after an arduous day's work (16 hours!) he invited some friends back for bridge and drinks. By midnight, they had all succumbed. Van Horne stayed up to determine the next day's course of action and, while doing so, consumed a bottle of brandy and a half-pound of caviar.

In 1885, during construction in the Rockies, a construction foreman foolishly asked him how he wanted the stations built. He replied, "Lots of logs there: cut them, peel them and build your stations." Thus it was with the first stations at Banff and Laggan (now Lake Louise). Eventually he succeeded George Stephen as president of the CPR and was knighted in 1894. When he died, the following was noted: "On September 11, 1915, his unjaded spirit reached its final terminal . . ."[7]

Equally as remarkable was George Stephen, the first president of the CPR (1881-1888). Born the son of a carpenter in Scotland in 1829, he emigrated to Canada in 1850. Rising swiftly in the entrepreneurial climate of the times, he also tied his fortunes to the Conservative party of John A. Macdonald. Stephen shared Macdonald's dream of a transcontinental railway. It was natural that he should become head of the fledgling Canadian Pacific Railway formed by the Tories in February of 1881. In 1886 a baronet was bestowed upon Stephen in recognition of his efforts, and in 1891 further honours came his way when he accepted a peerage with the title "Lord Mount Stephen." The title originated from a mountain named after him by the railway surveyors. He passed away in 1921. As evidence of their drive, both Stephen and Van Horne vowed that they could complete the railway in five years instead of the ten estimated previously.

Also worthy of mention is James Jerome Hill (1838-1916) of the Great Northern Railway. A little known fact is that this remarkable man was initially in charge of construction for the CPR syndicate. He was responsible for the appointments of Alpheus Stickney and Thomas A. Rosser as superintendent of construction and chief engineer respectively. In addition, he sent that "peppery master of picturesque profanity,"[8] Major A.B. Rogers, to search for the pass that now bears his name. Eventually, Hill split with Van Horne and Stephen over the route of the CPR. Hill wanted the line to avoid the costly route north of Lake Superior. He desired the CPR to connect with his railway, the St. Paul, Minneapolis and Manitoba Railway. As this would not be a purely Canadian route, it was rejected by the syndicate. Hill left the syndicate in May of 1883, vowing to see the CPR in hell "if he had to shovel coal to get there." This was the source of the later conflicts between the CPR and the GNR in the fight for control of southern British Columbia.

Another result of this battle was the departure of Stickney and Rosser, who did not measure up to the aggressive demands of Van Horne. Van Horne had assumed the role of general manager on January 2, 1882. In November of 1882, he recruited Thomas Shaughnesy as general purchasing agent. The previous system of favouritism soon disappeared as Shaughnesy demanded quality of material and price with favours to none. Now fine-tuned, the syndicate began to aggressively lay rail to the coast.

Chapter Two: Architectural Features of CPR Railway Stations

Until the 1940s, the railway station was the focal point of many B.C. communities. It dominated the town architecturally and socially. The building style of the railway station reflected the philosophy of the government of the day. The evolution from the older picturesque station to the modern avant-garde station demonstrates the change in railway architecture from prime exemplars of laissez-faire capitalism to the "international" style, signifying a society which in turn conceived of railroads primarily as a public service. The point is that there was a movement in station styles from individualistic stations unique to company, place and period, to a homogeneous national or federal design subsumed under the moderne or international style. This was in part influenced by, of all things, post offices and gas stations.

Although picturesque in style, the early railway station existed for one reason: to serve the needs of the railway. And it was constructed accordingly. "Picturesque" is defined as having "interesting asymmetrical dispositions of forms and variety of texture — as in the cottage *orne*."[9] Simply put, this means carved finials, decorative bargeboarding, wainscoting and similar motifs in a Victorian/Italianate manner. Railway officials decreed that the agent's family must live apart from the daily railroad operations. Thus, living quarters are almost invariably on the second storey. With the advent of the international style, this practice was largely abandoned. The transition in style is obvious if one compares the stations at Erikson and Creston, B.C. The picturesque station at the former community provided upstairs accommodation, while the station at Creston (1949) had no such provision.

The railway station is an example of that classic formula, "form follows function." A standard feature in every railway station is the bay window, which allowed the station agent to see up and down the line. In the construction of stations, cost savings were paramount, so a wood-siding finish was used almost exclusively. The soft, dark, tuscan-red colour was chosen for its durability, a characteristic owing to the high lead content in the paint. Original construction specifications did not include plumbing or electricity, although in some cases these were added later. For instance, the original Chemainus station, which had an agent until the mid-1950s, never did have washroom facilities. Most stations lacked a basement, so only a single stove was required for heat.

The uniformity of station design meant that the railway engineer could send a standard set of plans to any railway contractor-foremen, who would readily understand them. In turn, he would engage carpenters' assistants to complete the structure. Stations were erected in an assembly-line fashion: "The first gang put up the frame, joists and rafters. The second put on the sheeting, flooring and roofing. The third gang was comprised of plasterers, joiners and painters. Four or five stations were under construction at the same time. Uniformity of station design also prevented civic jealousy."[10] Quite simply, one town could not say it had a better station than another. If one compares the first Duncan and Nanaimo stations, the designs are nearly identical.

The railway stations of Vancouver Island are somewhat unusual in that there were two management phases. The Dunsmuir Syndicate owned the E & N until

1905, and the line only went as far as Wellington. On June 8 of that year, the CPR formally acquired the railway and, as the line was extended, began to imprint the new company standard station design on the Island. R.A. Bainbridge, CPR divisional engineer for the E & N following the CPR takeover, was chiefly responsible for the design of the Island stations. The small station at Bainbridge on the Port Alberni subdivision (now removed) was in all likelihood named after him. The original station at Port Alberni (1911) and those at Duncan (1912) and Courtenay (1914) are identical to many throughout the CPR system. Similar designs are also evident in the Parksville and Qualicum Beach stations.

Before we move on, let us examine the "international" style. The term was first introduced in a book by Henry-Russell Hitchcock in 1932. The style reached its apex in the 1930s, although political reaction and economic stagnation interrupted further development in several countries of Europe, notably Germany, Russia and France. However, by the late 1930s and into the 1950s, the international style had come to be almost universally accepted throughout the whole western world wherever modern technological advances were already an accomplished fact or even a relatively new importation.

The international style had its origins in the movements of the Bauhaus and Wermer schools of architecture, which rejected gaiety in design, favouring instead simplistic form. A good example of this contrast in styles is the CPR station at Coquitlam in contrast to the station at Fernie. The international style is characterized by corner windows and almost always has a flat roof. The picturesque canopy brackets of the earlier stations are absent, although the operator's bay survives in a modernistic fashion. Overall, the appearance is rectangular and almost clinical. Platforms of wood are replaced by concrete slabs. Silhouette-style lettering for station signs replaces the traditional sign, which usually hung below the eaves or was painted on the roof.

From the humble flagstops, such as Moberly in the Rockies, to the main terminals, such as Vancouver, every station performed an essential communication role. Prior to World War I, railways were the major form of transportation. The automobile had not yet achieved dominance, for a proper road network did not exist outside of the urban centres. On Vancouver Island, cars and trucks were frequently transported by the E & N over the Malahat prior to the road being improved. On the mainland, until the completion of the Hope-Princeton highway in 1949, road transport was carried by the Kettle Valley Railway. The loss of this source of revenue was a contributing factor to the eventual closure of the line. Travel by car was limited, and the distances travelled now would have been incomprehensible then.

The railway station was the centre of the economic and social life of the community, for here one received mail and freight and carried on business. Edwin P. Alexander wrote in his 1970 book, *Down at the Depot*, that "in those early days of the horse and buggy, the station was the only means of intercourse with the outside world."[11] For example, before the Esquimalt and Nanaimo Railway was built on Vancouver Island, the only reliable means of communication was by coastal steamer.

Railway stations frequently reflected the architectural style of the ethnic origins of a region. The CPR station at Castlegar was built in 1907, replacing an earlier one constructed in the same year but destroyed by fire. Now a museum, this station was built to the same plans as the original. It was characterized by a second storey with six indented dormers surrounding a hip roof. The first story had shingled eaves running the entire circumference of the building. The slanted dormers reflected a Germanic influence. An interesting variant was the absence of traditional bracket canopy supports. The station was not of the traditional board variety but was instead composed of individual letters above the roof line. A much larger station with a similar style is at Nelson. Here, we see traditional brackets for the awning and the signboard below the eaves.

With the exception of terminal stations such as Vancouver, masonry construction was not common. However, the Victoria E & N station constructed in 1887 was a variant. This station was a substantial one-storey masonry building. Vaguely Italian Renaissance in design, the Victoria terminus stood substantially unaltered until 1947 when a second storey was added and a new baggage and express facility was constructed behind the existing structure. Here, too, a new rectangular facade was imposed over the former picturesque exterior.

The most utilitarian station is the "flagstop" station. It consists of a bare wooden or cinder platform and a signboard. Some are enclosed on three sides, affording some protection from the elements. Examples on Vancouver Island are the platforms at Esquimalt and Starks. This type of station was known as a "flagstop" station because "the business handled by it was so light that a train would not stop to take passengers unless it had been 'flagged' by a hand or lantern signal . . ."[12] Disembarking passengers had to notify the conductor.

The type of station most common to British Columbia is the combined freight and passenger station. These are found at points where business handled is comparatively small, "and where in general it seems most desirable from economical and operating reasons to have all the station work done under a single roof."[13]

One interesting station type in the province was the resort-hotel station. In 1886 the CPR opened the first four such stations at Field, Glacier, Revelstoke and North Bend on its transcontinental line through the Rocky Mountains. "These four places were each located at the railway station, and they were primarily for the purpose of providing meals to train passengers as the railway grades were too heavy to justify the operation of dining cars through the mountains."[14] As the more efficient engines came on line, dining-car service was provided through the Rockies, and by 1936 meal service for train passengers had ceased at all four hotels. Cameron Lake and Strathcona Lodge on Vancouver Island were resort stations, although smaller than their mainland counterparts.

Interiors of the stations had many quirks that some would rather forget. For example, the curved station seats, which were so uncomfortable that most people preferred to stroll up and down the platform. Station doors provided a real obstacle, especially in winter. As you left to board the train, one of the two station doors swung inwards while the other hit you from behind. Some of the doors were fitted with spring hinges which made the exercise painful or acrobatic. Another quirk which we would find interesting was the advertising materials, posters and words of advice to travellers. "Advice to Young Girls Travelling Alone" was one example of the "thoughtful" writing provided by the railways.

Sometimes climate necessitated modification of the exterior design. Temperature control was often a problem, hence awnings and overhangs were introduced. These provided protection from both rain and summer heat. During the winter, the sun was still able to shine through the windows. Properly planted trees and the careful placement of the station to deflect the wind added a further degree of natural temperature control. The freight section of the station was often located so that it, rather than the office or waiting room, got the direct force of the prevailing winds.

While the design of smaller stations was for the most part not that interesting for the railway architects, it did call for some innovation to construct an efficient yet inexpensive structure. Credit must go to these men, as some of their stations are as solid today as the day they were built.

One interesting vignette of station lore is found in a 1928 CPR conductor's guide, which advises conductors to exercise caution when honouring tickets of stations with similar names. Examples cited include Abbotsford, B.C., and its counterpart in Quebec; Billings, B.C., and Billings, Ontario; and Vernon, B.C. and Verona, Ontario.

Except in the larger urban centres, the railway station is no longer a dominant structure. Elimination of passenger lines, centralized traffic control and other factors have all contributed to make the railway station little more than a picturesque vestige of a bygone era.

Chapter Three: Railway Stations by Division
Part One: Vancouver Island

The settlement patterns of Vancouver Island presaged the arrival of the railway. Steamship connections were in existence between such points as Victoria, Chemainus, Ladysmith and Nanaimo. However, the coming of the railway proved to be an economic catalyst in these areas. Indeed, the railway station became one of the focal points of the community. This is a fact difficult to realize today, but a glance at old city maps indicates the prominent location of stations. Today, as fate would have it, the Victoria and Duncan stations are still in central downtown locations.

The station at the foot of Pandora Avenue in Victoria is the fourth to serve as the southern terminus. Russell's station in Victoria West was the initial terminus. In 1887 a solid masonry station and a wooden freight shed were erected on Store Street in the downtown area, anticipating the arrival of the railway in 1888. The first passenger train arrived in Victoria on March 29 of that year. This structure, with alterations, stood at this location until 1972 when it was torn down to improve access to the Johnson Street bridge. At that time, a station was erected in Victoria West at the corner of Catherine Street and Esquimalt Road. Our present "cottage orne" station was built in 1985 on virtually the same location as its 1887 predecessor, so history has come full circle.

Farther up-Island, the station at Goldstream (mile 10.7), once an important stop, is gone. The Goldstream station served the adjacent area as well as being an arrival and departure point for guests at the old Goldstream Hotel. This hotel was a popular watering hole for Victoria residents, but it was frequently disparaged by local clergy. Dunsmuir's reply was that they should be grateful, as it removed the imbibers from town. In those days of steam, a water tower and section house were at Goldstream as well. The station also served the park itself, a popular Sunday destination point and the ideal spot for a picnic or a concert by Victoria's Fifth Regiment Band. This band still performs summer concerts at Fort Rodd Hill.

Malahat station (mile 20) has also been removed, but in the days of steam, it was a "pusher" station. Additional locomotives were often required to push trains from Victoria and Duncan over the Malahat.

In the early years of the railway, numerous large wooden trestles existed. An especially thrilling site was the magnificent trestle over Niagara Canyon (mile 14). By 1907 the CPR began upgrading the trestles and support facilities of the E & N. Many trestles were filled in, and others were replaced by steel structures. Originally wooden, the trestles at Niagara and Arbutus Canyons were replaced by substantial steel structures. The Niagara Canyon trestle was replaced in 1911 when the bridge formerly on the CPR mainline at Cisco Flats was moved to Niagara Canyon. This bridge was originally designed in New York, fabricated in San Francisco and placed in service on the CPR mainline in 1886. It was reinforced in 1940 at its present location. One may see this trestle by hiking a very steep trail from Goldstream Park.

Just south of Shawnigan Village at mile twenty-seven, the Canadian Pacific Railway had a resort station called Strathcona Hotel. Designed by Samuel Maclure, the hotel was built in 1900, and after changing hands several times, it was acquired by the CPR in 1916-17. Following its sale by the CPR in 1927, a girls' school was

Cont. on pg. 23

The first Strathcona Hotel was built in 1900 by a group called the Shawnigan Lake Hotel Company. Frederick T. Sherbourne was the contractor. On May 15, 1900, it burnt down, but was rebuilt immediately on the same plans by the same contractor. "The design is of Swiss architecture and was the work of Mr. Maclure of Victoria." A most commodious structure, it had thirty-two bedrooms in singles and suites and was located on fifty acres, eight of which were devoted to various pleasures such as croquet and tennis. After a series of owners, the CPR acquired the hotel in 1916-17. They operated it as a resort station until 1927, when it was sold and became a girls' school, although still remaining a stop on the line. The terminus was originally known as Gilesville, but in March of 1900, its name was changed on the railway timetable to Strathcona Hotel, and later, Strathcona Lodge. Following completion of the Strathcona Hotel, the stop simply became Strathcona.
Collection of the author.

Cowichan was one of the original stations on the E & N. It was reduced to flagstop status in the 1920s. The site is still a stop on the line, and this little station has been fixed up by local residents. In this June 6/71 photo, Train 51, Eng 8005, 8012, 30 cars and Van 436481 arrive at Cowichan Station. Trainman Dan Buchanan readies to dismount 8005 in preparation for picking up the two empty asphalt tanks. The Union Pacific auto-box actually went to Crofton in a rare movement from Victoria. Eng: Don MacLachan, Cdr: Jim Jordan.
Collection of John Hoffmeister.

Cont. from pg. 20

established in the hotel building, although it continued to be a scheduled stop for the railway. The structure was torn down in 1969.

At the resort centre of Shawnigan (mile 27.8), a VIA shelter serves as the railway station. This was once a very active station as it handled shipping for the Shawnigan Lake Lumber Company and other companies in the area. Until 1907, a commuter service ran in the summer to accommodate lake residents who worked in Victoria. In 1957 the station agent was removed, and the station was relegated to flagstop status.

In the Duncan area, stations at Cobble Hill (mile 31.2), Cowichan (mile 35.5) and Koksilah (mile 38.1) have long since been relegated to flagstop status or removed. The agent at Cobble Hill was removed in 1929. Stops are still made, although the older style flagstop stations have been replaced by VIA shelters.

Station gardens are another interesting aspect of our railway heritage. Although the gardens were in evidence on the mainland operations of the CPR for a long time, Vancouver Island did not receive its first formal station garden until 1909. The first garden was designed by A.E. Wallace of Victoria and was located at Duncan. Gardens were also established at Ladysmith, Lake Cowichan, Nanaimo, Parksville, Union Bay and Courtenay. In 1944 the agents were awarded prizes for their gardens.

From the beginning of rail service, mail was carried on the E & N. This service was provided until September 30, 1952. In the evenings, the mail car was left in the downtown yard so one could post a letter to, say, Duncan, and it would arrive the following day. Certainly an improvement on today's service. A former mail clerk on the E & N was Arthur L. Robinson, who served on the mail trains from 1916-1952. At the time of writing, Arthur (Robbie) Robinson lives in a senior citizens' centre in Victoria.

Duncan, at mile 39.7, received its first station in 1887 but not until after a protest by residents of the community then called "Duncan's." (Prior to this, it was known as Alderlea.) When Prime Minister Macdonald was making his inaugural trip on the Esquimalt and Nanaimo Railway with President Dunsmuir, a delegation halted the train at Duncan's Crossing. They presented their demands for a station,

and Dunsmuir acceded to their request. In 1912 the present station was constructed, replacing the 1887 structure. The Duncan station recently received a new lease on life and has been restored with the aid of a provincial Heritage Trust grant. It is now a designated heritage building.

The flagstop stations at the communities of Stratford's Crossing (mile 44.4) and Westholme (mile 47) have long since disappeared, and these places are no longer scheduled stops on the E & N.

Chemainus (mile 51.2) is the next station, the oldest extant, albeit altered, station on Vancouver Island when it was removed in 1982. It was constructed in 1886 under the supervision of Mr. W.E. Blackett. The station at the former flagstop of Somenos (mile 43) was refurbished to take on a new role as the Chemainus flagstop station.

Ladysmith (mile 58.4) was originally called Oyster Harbour. The first station was built in 1901 and removed in 1944. A contemporary newspaper account described the new station as a "conventional one-story cottage design, completely modern in finish."[15] Ladysmith was once a "transfer point" to the mainland. With the creation of the Wellcox yards at Nanaimo in 1955, the transfer site at Ladysmith was abandoned. It eventually became a recreational area, and is now known as Transfer Park. Adjacent to the railway station were the offices of Crown Zellerbach Logging, which operated a logging railway to the Nanaimo Lakes. This operation was closed down in 1987, and most of their rolling stock was donated to the Ladysmith Historical Railway Society, who hope to inaugurate steam excursion rides to the "Lakes."

At mile 68, the former coal-mining community of South Wellington languishes among the slag heaps of the past. Here, one may follow the abandoned grade of the Pacific Coast Collieries Railroad to Boat Harbour some seven miles distant and enjoy a picnic at this once-important shipping point.

The railway station at Nanaimo (mile 72.5) is the second to serve the city. Construction of the first Nanaimo railway station began in July of 1885. The *Nanaimo Free Press* of July 18, 1885, reported that "the depot, which will be large and commodious, will be erected between Franklyn and Fitzwilliam streets."[16] Mr. W.E. Blackett again supervised construction. E & N

Cont. on pg. 31

Until September 30, 1952, mail was handled on the E & N. In these two photographs, Arthur L. Robinson, mail clerk on the railway from 1916-1952, is shown sorting the mail and passing out the last bag on September 30, 1952. Courtesy of A.L. Robinson.

Virtually isolated until the railway arrived, Lake Cowichan became one of Vancouver Island's prime timber areas following completion of the line in 1913. The contract for building a section house and station house was awarded to a local resident, Mr. George Bishop. Another resident, Jim Palmer, assisted in the construction. The first passenger train arrived on June 18, 1913, bearing local dignitaries, most prominent of whom were Mayor Duncan of the city of that name, and members of his council. Mr. Corbett was the first station agent. Passenger service was discontinued on April 21, 1926. In 1976 the station was removed from service and is now the local museum under the auspices of the Kaatza Historical Society.

This photo shows C.P. Rail Extra 8643-8613 West with a 32-car consist of empty log skeleton flatcars entering Lake Cowichan. Mile 18.0 Lake Cowichan subdivision at 9:15 a.m. 3-11-75.

Photo by Dave Wilkie.

*A view of the Chemainus station in 1944. When the CPR acquired the railway in 1905, they replaced and/or altered many of the stations. As the automobile became the dominant form of transportation, the station deteriorated and the agent was removed in the late 1950s. Finally, it was demolished in 1983.
Victoria City Archives: 97803-01.*

The Esquimalt and Nanaimo Railway station at Wellington was built in 1887, the year Dunsmuir extended the line. This was the site of the headquarters of the E & N until 1913 when the shops were moved to their present location. Wellington was named after the Duke of Wellington (of Waterloo fame) and a former British Prime Minister (1828-1830). This structure typifies the architectural style of the Dunsmuir-era stations.
Canadian Pacific Corporate Archives: A19458.

The Cameron Lake Chalet was built in 1912. It was one of the CPR resort stations on the Island (the other being Strathcona Lodge) and was open from May 1 to October 15. Passenger service ceased in 1957. After a series of managers, it closed its doors in 1966.
Alberni Valley Museum: PN 2586.

In 1898 Dunsmuir extended his coal holdings into Cumberland. The railway extended to Union Bay where ships from all over the world loaded coal from Dunsmuir's mines. The railway station at Cumberland was actually the general store of Simon Leiser, a local merchant. Standing until recently, it was described as having "a very imposing false front set off by steeples or minarets at either end . . . the very latest thing in 1890 western architecture." When the CPR took over the E & N in 1905 and extended the line to Courtenay in 1914, an interchange was provided at Royston. Passenger service ceased in 1933.
Cumberland Museum: C 30-12.

Cont. from pg. 23

officials must have been pleased with Mr. Blackett for he was in charge of all the stations from Nanaimo to Esquimalt. The contract for painting the stations was awarded to a Mr. Louis Page. It was noted in the Nanaimo newspaper of September 18, 1886, that Mr. Page, "having secured the contract for painting the station houses on the Island line, has a large force of painters at work, so as to have them complete when the line opens for traffic on October 1."

Hotels were frequently constructed in proximity to the railway stations. At Duncan, the Quamichan Hotel was a frequent stop for railway travellers. Contiguous to the Nanaimo station was the Occidental Hotel. This establishment, which is still in business, was erected by Mr. Samuel Fiddick in 1886-87. A contemporary newspaper account described it as a "commodious and handsome two storey brick hotel . . . furnished throughout in the most modern style."

The present Nanaimo station was built in 1920 to replace the 1886 structure and is perhaps the most striking example of railway architecture on the Island. Its shingled base forms a pleasant contrast to its half-timbered upper storey. Spacious living quarters were provided for the agent and his family upstairs, while a large waiting room and baggage area were provided for passengers. The original freight shed still stands, although it is now in private hands. A local heritage group has restored the station's neglected exterior, and the building has become a designated heritage structure.

Wellington, at mile 77.3, was once the northern terminus, and the railway had a roundhouse and full support facilities here. It was originally mile 0. With the removal of the terminus to Victoria in 1913, it declined in importance so that now only a solitary nameboard is evidence of this historic site.

At Nanoose Bay, just beyond Nanaimo, one may see rotting pilings in the bay. This was the site of the Straits Lumber Company, which had a sawmill at this location. Locally known as Redgap after the mountain overlooking the bay, this mill ceased operations in October of 1942 because of a log shortage. It straddled both sides of the track, necessitating the locomotive to go right into the mill to pick up the freight cars. Shipping to off-Island points was handled at Jayem (mile 84.5). This was a transfer point to the mainland until 1955, when it suffered the same fate as the Ladysmith transfer point and was abandoned.

Four miles south of Parksville, a station stood at a junction called Craig's Crossing (mile 92). The nameboard on the station read "Craig." With its picturesque bellcast roof, it served as a passenger shelter and distribution point for local freight.

Parksville station (mile 95.2) was built in 1910. It is unique in that it still has a water tower, the only one on the Island. In 1982 the operator was removed, but it is still an important terminus for freight and passenger traffic as it is on the junction of the line to Port Alberni. This complex once had an adjacent restaurant building which was situated between the water tower and the station. The next station on the line, at Qualicum Beach (mile 101.8), still serves this resort community. It was built in 1913, and a vestigial remnant of its station garden still exists behind a red picket fence.

Between here and Courtenay, the many flagstop stations have long since fallen to the wrecker's hammer.

At mile 139.7, the line terminates at Courtenay. The station was built in 1914. An interesting feature is its separate ladies' and mens' waiting rooms.

In addition to the building program undertaken by the CPR in 1907, extensions to the present network were built. An eighteen-mile line was constructed to Lake Cowichan, a community some twenty miles from Duncan. Passenger service was inaugurated on June 18, 1913. It was scheduled thrice weekly on Wednesday, Saturday and Sunday. The service was not successful and was withdrawn on April 21, 1926. This line had wayside stations similar to those on other parts of the system.

In 1911 the CPR laid rail to the twin cities of Port Alberni and Alberni. The station at Port Alberni is the only extant station on this line. Many flagstop stations did exist, as the timetable shows, but when passenger service stopped in 1957, their importance quickly diminished. It should also be mentioned that the last major extension on the CPR was constructed in this area. In 1925 the railway built a branch line from Solly Junction near Port Alberni to Great Central Lake to extract lumber. This line carried no passengers and was torn up in 1953.

Passenger service still exists on Vancouver Island, but at present, the matter is before the courts because of federal and provincial differences of opinion regarding the E & N land grant and the promise of rail service in perpetuity.

Part Two: Vancouver

With the formation of the CPR Syndicate, and under the terms of the 1881 contract, Prime Minister Macdonald decreed that Port Moody was to be the western terminus of the CPR. Under the Onderdonk contract, the section between Port Moody and Savona was completed by late 1884, and in 1885 Onderdonk inaugurated a weekly passenger and freight service between those two points. On July 1, 1886, he turned this section over to the CPR. The first through passenger train arrived on July 4, 1886, at 12:00 noon at the western terminus of Port Moody.

However, Port Moody's time in the sun as the western terminus of the CPR was to be brief. It soon became readily apparent that the site at the head of Burrard Inlet. When John A. Macdonald decided on commercial development. Land had originally been ceded to the federal government from the province for provision of a railway terminus along False Creek and Burrard Inlet. When John A. MacDonald decided on Port Moody as the railway's terminus, the lands reverted to the province. Van Horne, seeing the obvious advantages of extending the line, began negotiations with the province which resulted in an arrangement that the CPR receive a total land grant of approximately 6,458 acres, including some private donations. In return, the CPR agreed to build a major hotel and opera house. The distance between Port Moody and the yet unnamed terminus was only twelve miles.

All that was left was to name the newly selected site. Van Horne's favourite literature was that which depicted explorers and exploration. So as John Murray Gibbon stated in his fine work, *Steel of Empire*, it was natural that he should select for the Pacific terminal "of a transcontinental railway, conceived and carried out with such bold enterprise"[17] the name of the great adventurer and explorer, Vancouver. Prior to this, the site was a sleepy village known as Coal Harbour which had been devastated by fire just two weeks prior to the arrival of the first transcontinental train. Construction of the line from Port Moody proceeded quickly, and on May 23, 1887, just a day before Queen Victoria's birthday and her Silver Jubilee, the first CPR train reached the port of Vancouver. It was a truly festive occasion, celebrating these two great events. In true Victorian pomp and ceremony, the locomotive carried a picture of the beloved monarch, and slogans such as "Montreal-Vancouver" were cheered as the train passed under the ceremonial arch.

The first CPR station at Vancouver was a very modest structure, seemingly out of place with the greatness of the occasion. However, it showed the financial acumen of the CPR. They would build a more substantial terminal when traffic potential warranted. It was not long in coming.

On August 7, 1888, Van Horne became president of the CPR, and with the same enthusiasm he showed in the construction days, he now channelled his energies toward aggressive commercialization. In the first year of Vancouver's role as the Pacific terminus, the town's population rose to 7,000. In 1886-87, the CPR extended its line to New Westminster, once the capital of the province. The station at New Westminster (1898), designed by Edward Maxwell, still stands, although it does not perform its original function.

At Huntingdon on the U.S. border, a line was laid to Mission in 1889, thereby securing access to the U.S. at

Cont. on pg. 46

Vancouver received its first station in 1887 upon extension of the line from Port Moody. Vancouver's second station was completed in 1898 and was designed by Edward Maxwell. Its most notable feature was the two towers supplanted over a romanesque archway. The building had a remarkably short lifespan and was removed in 1914.
Collection of the author.

Vancouver's third station was designed by the architectural firm of Barrott, Blackader and Webster. Constructed in true classical proportions during the years 1912-1914, it now has a new role as a shopping arcade in addition to serving as the terminus for the seabus to the north shore.
Collection of the author.

This early photograph shows the CPR station at Clayburn on the junction with the British Columbia Electric railway, whose station is to the left. The Clayburn station was removed in the 1920s. British Columbia Hydro Archives.

Port Moody was the first coastal terminus of the CPR. This small mansard roof structure was completed in 1886 and received the first transcontinental train on July 4, 1886. In 1887 the terminus moved to Vancouver, and this station still operated, although in reduced status. It was replaced in 1905. After having served as an office building for Gulf Oil Canada, this historic structure was finally torn down in 1961, and the only surviving memento is the brass chandelier in the Port Moody City Hall.
Canadian Pacific Corporate Archives: A7632

The station at New Westminster was designed by architect Edward Maxwell and was built in 1898-1899, replacing the original 1886 structure. With completion of the new station, the name of the site was changed from Westminster Junction to New Westminster. A very picturesque structure, it shares design similarities with CPR stations at Vernon and Red Deer, Alberta. BCARS: F 82-78.

This station at Hammond was built in 1912, replacing the 1883 structure, which was moved down the track to become a warehouse. The same year the new station opened, the agent and his assistant won first prize for the best kept station and station garden in B.C. Passenger trains last stopped here in 1959, and it has since been removed. The name was derived from two residents, John and William Hammond, who owned the townsite.
BCARS: C-5846.

Named after an early settler, Thomas Haney, this station was erected in 1933. A picturesque structure, it boasts a bellcast roof, curved station benches and a wooden platform. The well-tended station garden is evidence of the agent's pride in his station. The building has since been removed.
BCARS: F-2543.

The original station at this point was called Mission Junction when the railway built a branch line to Sumas, Washington. Constructed in 1886, this structure typifies the early CPR design with the contrasting siding in the upper and lower storeys, Swiss chalet gable ends and the diagonal sheathing below the windows.
Canadian Pacific Corporate Archives: A17775.

Built in 1909, this station replaced the original structure. The name was changed to Mission City and, since 1973, has simply become Mission. This building is evocative of the English Domestic Revival style with the timbering in the upper storey. It still serves as a divisional point and passenger stop.
Collection of the author.

This 1907 photograph shows the station and support facilities at Harrison Mills. Originally called Harrison Siding, the railway adopted the townsite's name in 1912. It took its name from Benjamin Harrison, a Quaker, who was deputy governor of the Hudson's Bay Company from 1835-1839. It was torn down in the 1960s. The store in the extreme right is now a museum and is well worth a visit for information on the area. Kilbey Historic Park Museum: K 975.17.6.

The station at Agassiz was built in 1893. For many years, dining cars were detached here from westbound trains and attached to eastbound trains. This was also the "jumping-off point" for Harrison Hot Springs, and a stage jitney met train passengers bound for the Springs. In September 1907, the CPR inaugurated a daily Agassiz-Vancouver service which was very well received. Insul-brick siding was added to the structure in the 1940s to reduce maintenance and heating costs. The site was named after Captain Lewis N. Agassiz of the Royal Welsh Fusiliers, who settled in this district in 1867.
Canadian Pacific Corporate Archives: A17755.

Ruby Creek, B.C. (1900). Long since removed, this station is shown with the agent, his wife and the station crew with their velocipede. Until 1958 this small community was without road access. Frustrated by a lack of government cooperation, local residents constructed their own road. This station was removed in the late 1960s.
Canadian Pacific Corporate Archives: A 17752.

The CPR hotel at North Bend was named Fraser Canyon House and was opened for service in 1887. It shared similar architectural features with its counterparts at Field and Glacier.
BCARS: D-1495.

Cont. from pg. 32

Sumas, thence to the American network of rail lines. Constructed in 1912, the Mission station still stands, replacing the original structure from when this stop was called Mission Junction. Vancouver was now booming due to the diversification of its economy. Tea ships from the Orient, consigned by merchants in Montreal, were a romantic and profitable part of early CPR trade. Lumber and fish exports, via rail to the east and by CPR ships across the Pacific, fattened the CPR coffers. Every small station in the lower mainland throbbed with activity as trains moved local products. Freight, with diverse cargoes such as sugar beets and whale oil, filled the waybills of the station agents. Commuter traffic had its origins in these times. In 1907 a daily commuter service was offered between Vancouver and Agassiz.

A report issued by the Vancouver Board of Trade in 1888 showed that the CPR expended $648,234.65 in that year, and this figure was to be exceeded by $144,500 in 1889. Freight traffic showed 21,441 tons of goods shipped east in 1887, while 38,895 tons arrived. With the understatement typical of reports in those days, it concluded the following: "The Railroad situation as compared with that of twelve months ago may be decidedly declared as 'developing.'"[18] This was an era of unparalleled growth and opportunity, soon to be overcome by the horror and agony of World War I.

This station at Spence's Bridge was built in 1952, replacing the original structure. It is an excellent exemplar of the international style with its flat roof, lack of awning supports and overall rectangular appearance. The site was named after Thomas Spence, who built a toll-bridge to replace the ferry crossing. After the Coquihalla route was abandoned in 1959, passenger and freight trains were routed via Spence's Bridge to the mainline.
Collection of the author.

Part Three: Kettle Valley

The Kettle Valley Railway was the CPR artery in the Okanagan and was opened for through service on July 31, 1916. An announcement in the *Vancouver Sun* of July 28, 1916, read as follows: "The Canadian Pacific Railway announces their new service to Nelson via Hope, effective July 31, 1916, service daily. An important feature in this connection is a through sleeper to Nelson, as well as day coach and cafe and dining car accommodation."[19] Thus began a rail passenger service from Vancouver across southern British Columbia which was to survive until the last run on January 17, 1964.

With the rail line completed between Procter and Kootenay Landing in 1930, rail transport was secured across the entire southern half of the province. To step back in time, Van Horne was justifiably aware of the threat of the Great Northern. He made a visit to the Columbia and Kootenay Railway and Navigation Company, which linked Robson and Nelson and was built to stem the southerly flow of ore south down the Columbia to Little Dalles. Indeed, once the company acquired this operation, it became quite obvious that "the CPR's C & K branch was ineffectual in reversing more than a marginal volume of Kootenay ore flowing to the United States."[20]

Shortly after his return to Montreal, Van Horne personally assigned engineer J.A. Coryell to begin surveying a railway route from the C & K at Robson to the Fraser River and the CPR mainline at Hope. To further exacerbate the situation, in 1893 the second of the northwest American lines, the Great Northern, was completed. The first line had been established with the meeting of the rails of the Union Pacific and the Central Pacific at Promontory, Utah, in 1869. (For the purpose of assuaging Canadian pride, it must be noted that these two American lines were not transcontinental in the Canadian sense for they did not possess an unbroken line of track from sea to sea as did the CPR.) As events would have it, a severe depression struck in 1893-94, and this fact, coupled with the worst flooding in the area that the CPR had ever experienced, delayed construction until 1895.

Thomas Shaughnesy succeeded Van Horne in June, 1899, and over the winter, the railway pushed west from Robson, reaching Grand Forks on September 18, 1899. By 1900 the CPR had reached Midway and extended a branch line from Eholt to Phoenix to tap the extensive ore bodies in that region. The Great Northern had a line here also. Strangely enough during this period, Great Northern President J.J. Hill did not move to counteract the western thrust of the CPR. These were strange times. Shaughnesy announced that the CPR would halt at Midway for the foreseeable future, yet in January of 1900, a group of CPR surveyors struggled into Hope, having surveyed the CPR line from Midway to Hope. Van Horne's directive had been carried out. "On the streets of Vancouver, general widespread praise of the CPR was to be heard for the first time in more than a decade."[21]

Following numerous negotiations with the provincial governments of the day, and a decade after the first surveys, construction began in 1911. Constructed throughout 1911-1915, the Kettle Valley Railway was an engineering marvel of its time and a triumph for the chief engineer, Andrew McCulloch. This remarkable man was born in Lanark County, Ontario, on June 16, 1864. He had much experience in railways, having been division engineer of construction for the eastern lines of the CPR,

Cont. on pg. 51

Before the Coquihalla Pass was abandoned in 1959, and a subsequent decision was made to route traffic over the Windermere subdivision to the mainline at Golden and thence to the coast, the Penticton station was a focal point of CPR operations in southern B.C. Originally, the terminus was on the shore of Lake Okanagan at the foot of Martin Street in downtown Penticton. Here, passengers alighted from the S.S. Sicamous from Okanagan Landing and other points, or from eastern and western points on the KVR system. The Incola Hotel, operated by the CPR, served the needs of passengers. With the demise of the sternwheelers, the station's location became redundant. Accordingly, a new structure was erected on Fairview Road in 1941 and opened for service on December 15 of that year. As in the Mission station, the tudor-style timbering is reminiscent of the English Domestic Revival style. This station is now closed and at the time of writing was up for sale.
Penticton Museum.

This photograph shows the sternwheeler Aberdeen at the railway station, waiting for train passengers bound for communities along Okanagan Lake. Its destination is Okanagan Landing where passengers can transfer to trains for mainline connections.

49

A typical day at the lakeshore station with the arrival of the passenger train.

Cont. from pg. 48

headquartered in Montreal. However, his heart belonged in the West, and in his early days, he worked on numerous CPR construction gangs, one of which was on the CPR line between Nakusp and Slocan. When the decision to construct the Kettle Valley was finally made, it was logical that CPR President Thomas Shaughnesy would select Andrew McCulloch as its chief engineer.

McCulloch's second in charge was J.J. Warren, a gentleman of the same ilk. Upon their arrival in Penticton in June of 1910, they were confronted by a myriad of problems. Construction had been intermittent over the years, and the indefatigable J.J. Hill was breathing down their necks with his Victoria, Vancouver & Eastern Railway. Hill had powerful allies in the British Columbia legislature who would not have been displeased if the CPR failed in its objectives. His tracks had already reached Princeton, having passed through Keremeos and Hedley from Oroville on the Washington-B.C. border. The *bete-noire* of Van Horne was now poised to push his line through to the desirable coal country of Tulameen and Coalmount.

After six years of challenging and difficult ordeals, the first Kettle Valley passenger train reached Penticton on May 31, 1915. Through service was available from Midway to Merritt. The Coquihalla remained to be conquered, and it is here that the true genius of McCulloch came to the forefront. The Quintette Tunnels, five miles west of Hope, are one of the world's monuments to engineering genius. Eric Sismey describes them best in an article written for the *Islander* in 1964: "Near Othello, five miles above Hope, a marvel of engineering and construction, the Quintette Tunnels, were drilled; five in perfect alignment, and between each one, the Coquihalla zigged and zagged under steel spans."[22] This section was completed, and the line was opened for through traffic in 1916.

Compromise was finally reached between the warring CPR and GNR. Due to wartime exigencies, and perhaps also due to a growing weariness of all the bickering, the stretch of railway between Brookmere and Princeton had been undertaken as a joint effort. Upon completion of the line, the Great Northern only ran one train over it, and Louis J. Hill, who had succeeded his father as president of the railway, rode this train as a tribute to his father's perseverance in pushing the line through. The agreement with the Great Northern terminated in 1944 when the CPR purchased running rights over the entire line.

Architectural evidence of the Great Northern's former presence remains in three of the line's stations: Brookmere (1915), Tulameen (1915) and Princeton (1909). These one-storey structures with their boxed eaves were all still extant at the time of writing. The Brookmere station houses an art gallery, the Tulameen station is a private residence and the Princeton station, although boarded up, still serves the railway.

The town of Princeton has an interesting railway history. It was named after Edward, Prince of Wales, who had made a Royal Tour in 1861 and was King-Emperor from 1901-1910. This sleepy southern British Columbia town was once the junction of three railways: the branch line to Copper Mountain, the CPR line from Penticton and the Great Northern from the United States. The Copper Mountain spur was removed in 1958, while the Great Northern trackage was ripped up in 1939. The roadbed now forms part of southern British Columbia's Highway 3.

From Princeton, the Kettle Valley line winds uphill to Osprey Lake, 3,592 feet above sea level, before beginning the slow descent to Penticton. Construction of this section posed great difficulty, especially the bridging of Trout Creek, which was the highest bridge on the Kettle Valley Railway. Once again, McCulloch displayed his skills. He overruled four engineers regarding the length of a steel span and with his assistant, Michael McKay, resurveyed the canyon. His figuring proved correct, for when the steel span was lowered into position, it was only 1/4 inch short of a perfect fit.

Nine-and-a-half miles from Penticton is the site of the former West Summerland station. Before being removed, this station housed a museum of KVR memorabilia. The Penticton station is the second one to service the fruit capital of British Columbia. The first station was erected in 1912 and was on the lakeshore at the foot of Martin Street. Nearby was the Incola Hotel, CPR-owned, which served weary rail and steamboat passengers.

Until 1936 the CPR steamship *S.S. Sicamous* plied the waters of Okanagan Lake. In 1931 the CPR constructed a line from Penticton to Okanagan Falls,

Cont. on pg. 62

The station on Fairview Road, which opened for service on December 15, 1941.

The station at West Summerland was built in 1923 and has since been removed. It was designed in a style evocative of the Mediterranean with its white plaster facade and spacious appearance. Altogether, a very pleasing style in harmony with the salubrious sunny climate of the Okanagan.
Penticton Museum.

The Kettle Valley Railway reached Oliver in 1923, the year the station was built. In 1979 permission was granted to discontinue service, and the rails were lifted shortly thereafter. After remaining abandoned for some years, the station has been tastefully restored as a museum.
Collection of the author.

54

The last extension of the KVR was in 1944, when the line reached Osoyoos. Reefer cars of fruit and produce were the main commodities shipped over this section, but with trucks increasingly used for transport of such goods, the CPR applied for abandonment of the line. It was granted, and the tracks were lifted in 1979. Collection of the author.

In 1892 the Shuswap and Okanagan Railway was completed between Sicamous and Vernon. Steamship service was provided to Penticton and lakeshore communities en route. The station at Okanagan landing, shown in 1916, still exists as a private dwelling. Canadian Pacific Corporate Archives: A2915.

Okanagan Landing (private residence).
Courtesy of Ned Hanning.

The station at Tulameen was built in 1915. The architectural style is that of the Great Northern, for they constructed this part of the line. Until 1925, nearby Otter Lake was a source of ice used by the Great Northern Railway. This station is now a private residence. Collection of the author.

It seems in this photograph that the only thing keeping the train from falling into the station are the rail ties propping up the engine! The Jellicoe station was on the line between Princeton and Penticton and was named after Admiral Jellicoe of British naval fame during World War I.
Penticton Museum.

The station at Brookmere was built in 1915 and closed for service on August 1, 1965, when the CPR moved its divisional point to Merritt. This was a unique station in that it served both Great Northern and CPR trains under the Coquihalla agreement which saw both railways share this section of the line. The station had two operator's bays for the needs of each railway while the water tower had two spouts! The station now has new life as an arts centre.
Collection of the author.

Located on the Merritt subdivision, the Nicola station was built in 1907 and has since been removed. Initially, it was thought the railway would be extended to Kamloops and Nicola would become an important railway centre. Instead, only a branch line extended to Nicola with the result being that Merritt became the predominant community while Nicola languished at the end of a spur line.
Canadian Pacific Corporate Archives: A19555.

Cont. from pg. 51

thereby eliminating barge service on Skaha Lake. The present station on Fairview Road was erected in 1941 and is now boarded up and for sale. Once the transportation hub of southern British Columbia, Penticton is no longer accessible by passenger rail or steamer service. The *S.S. Sicamous* languishes on the shore of Lake Okanagan, perhaps waiting to steam again.

Rail travel to Penticton died a slow death. The decline had set in with the completion of the Hope-Princeton highway in 1949. The last major extension of the Kettle Valley Railway was in 1944 when the line was extended from Okanagan Falls to Osoyoos. Stations are still extant at Oliver and Osoyoos. The station at Oliver is a museum, while the Osoyoos station serves as a yacht club. This line was constructed to transport fruit crops and was in part necessitated by wartime fuel rationing. It has since been removed.

A severe snowstorm caused the unofficial abandonment of the Coquihalla Pass route in November of 1959. This, coupled with declining revenues and the burgeoning costs of keeping the railway open during the severe winters, caused the CPR to apply for official abandonment, which was granted by the Board of Transport on July 19, 1961. Snowfall averaged 469 inches during the winter months on the Coquihalla. Passenger use was already in decline and now was further strained by the fact that the railroad diverted traffic up the main line to Spence's Bridge. There, the cars were shifted onto the Nicola Valley line, which connected with the eastern end of the Coquihalla line at Brodie. Train passengers had to transfer at 2:35 a.m. to a Budd car for Penticton and other eastern points. Understandably, this inconvenience caused a decline in ridership.

Despite the awkwardness of the route's schedule, its natural attractions provided compensation. The traveller was often rewarded with a view of dawn breaking over the shimmering vista of the Tulameen River Valley. This view was even more spectacular in the fall with the changing of the leaves. Sadly, the inevitable happened. Declining patronage caused the CPR to apply for discontinuance of passenger service. The last run was on January 17, 1964. In June of 1990 permission was granted by the Canadian Transport Commission to abandon the line between Spence's Bridge and Penticton.

Part Four: Kootenay

The year 1893 saw an economic depression descend over the new Dominion, and of course, this affected the fortunes of the CPR and the Great Northern. The economic downturn caused Hill to strengthen his push for feeder lines into southern British Columbia. Van Horne was determined to deny his arch-rival the wealth of this area. He saw the competition at the Great Northern as "hungry hounds ready to jump in!"[23]

The CPR extended its line from Revelstoke to Wigwam in 1893. The terminus remained there until 1895 when the line was extended to the community of Arrowhead. This line was known as the Revelstoke and Arrow Lake Branch. Competition now reached a fever pitch as the CPR and the GN aimed for the heart of the Slocan mining district. Hill began his Kaslo and Slocan Railway, starting at Kaslo and reaching Sandon on October 23, 1895. Not far behind was the Nakusp and Slocan Railway, a subsidiary of the CPR, which reached Three Forks by the end of 1894, and finally Sandon on December 12, 1895. The stations along this line were described as follows: "At Nakusp there is a very good station with waiting rooms, baggage room and office on the ground floor and living apartments above . . . At Rosebury, a combined passenger station and freight shed has been built. At Three Forks there is a good passenger station and a large freight shed. All these buildings are of wood, are painted and completed."[24]

Meanwhile, further south, disagreements arose between American mining promoters Corbin and Augustus Heinze regarding the use of Corbin's rail line (the Nelson and Fort Sheppard) for the transport of refined ore to the smelters at Spokane. These disagreements resulted in Heinze's construction of a smelter at Trail and the construction of the Trail Creek Tramway. "While this little line may not have been particularly impressive compared to the larger standard gauge railroads, it was given a warm welcome by the citizens of both Trail and Rossland. In service early in 1896, it immediately became an important trade and travel route."[25]

Pleased with his success in this venture, Heinze extended his line to Robson West in 1897 where he effected a connection with the CPR, which had recently acquired the charter of the Columbia and Kootenay Railway. With the construction of the line from Slocan to Slocan Junction being completed by December 1, 1897, and with the Red Mountain Railway in place from the mines at Rossland to Northport, Corbin was shut out, and the cards were soon to be in the hands of the CPR. By 1897 the CPR had acquired all of Corbin's lines in B.C.

In 1897 the right to build a railway through the Crowsnest Pass was granted to the Canadian Pacific Railway. One factor contingent on this charter was a piece of legislation known as the "Crow Rate." In fact, this was in force until 1983. From this charter, the CPR received a subsidy of $3,381,000 and the right to select six square miles of coal lands tributary to the Crow's Nest Line in British Columbia.[26] With completion of the line in 1898 came a truly remarkable flow of settlers. Coal was king. Railways required it, and domestic and industrial consumption boomed as well.

Towns such as Natal and Michel, now gone except for the railway station at Natal (recently removed) and the hotel at the latter, satisfied demands for labour and ancillary industries. They were boom years, and the CPR

Cont. on pg. 82

Fernie CPR. Construction of the present CPR station at Fernie commenced on October 31, 1908, and the building was ready for occupancy on February 1, 1909. The Victoria Times *described it as "handsome and very commodious. The waiting rooms, baggage and express offices are large and airy, and the agent's and operator's quarters all that could be desired."*

Surprisingly, the station at Natal survived into the 1980s. The coal trains pass here before heading up the Windermere subdivision and on to Roberts Bank. This station is typical of the standard combined freight and passenger type.
Courtesy of the author.

Nestled in the heart of the coal belt, the railway station at Michel was built in 1898, the year the CPR completed its Crow's Nest line. With dieselization and the discontinuance of passenger service in 1964, these communities declined in importance. In the same year a decision was reached to centre coal operations at a new town called Sparwood, resulting in the razing of Michel and the neighbouring town of Natal. The station at Michel has long since gone, although the hotel still remains.
Canadian Pacific Corporate Archives: A 19112.

Cranbrook has had an interesting history in regard to railway station construction. The first Cranbrook station was built in 1898. When it became evident that a larger station was needed, a decision was taken to enlarge the structure. However, during construction, a terrible accident occurred. The Cranbrook Herald of May 25, 1905, reported that: "At 10:50 last Tuesday morning, the second storey of the CPR station that was being jacked up to admit the construction of a third storey fell without a moment's warning, catching all of the men working beneath." The railway company provided assistance on the spot, and with the full effort of the community, further tragedy was avoided and construction proceeded after the needs of the injured were attended to.
Canadian Pacific Corporate Archives: A 13030.

First station after the accident and addition of the additional storey.

The present Cranbrook station. It was designed by Le Corbusier and follows the architectural precepts of the International style. Believe it or not, this is actually the old station remodelled!
BCARS: photo number 23139.

In 1898 construction of the Crows Nest Branch from Lethbridge was completed. These stations featured a high "A" shaped dormer on the front with eight-foot overhangs. The station at Aldridge was named after W.H. Aldridge, manager of the Canadian Smelting Works.
Canadian Pacific Corporate Archives: A 13014.

Erected in 1901, this station served Kimberley until 1968. It features a mansard roof. The insul-brick siding obvious in this photo was added to many CPR stations in the 1940s to reduce maintenance costs. This station has a new life as a restaurant, the first railway station in B.C. so converted.
BCARS: F-8280.

The CPR station at Yahk was built in 1912 and cost $6,000, according to a local resident. This station was important in the early days for it was a link to Spokane, Washington, and the American rail network. This photo shows CPR Rail Passenger Extra BCR 2860 West entering Yahk, B.C. Mile 40.6 Nelson subdivision at 1:23 p.m., 3-30-79, with the Province of B.C.'s "Good Times '79 Express," en route to the Spokane World Fair.
Photo by Dave Wilkie.

The "Crowsnest" style station at Kitchener (now McConnel). The agent and his family are posed for the photograph, while a train passenger looks on. The section crew are with their velocipede.
Canadian Pacific Corporate Archives: A 12999.

In 1930 the CPR completed its extension from Procter to Kootenay Landing, thereby eliminating the need for sternwheeler service between these two points. By way of this line, a link-up to the Crow's Nest Pass Railway was effected at Sirdar near Creston. Needless to say, this station has also been removed.
BCARS: A 3851.

Built in 1895, the Kaslo station was the eastern terminus of the Kaslo-Slocan Railway. Freight and passengers went from here to Nelson and other way-points by CPR sternwheelers. The stations of the K & S have been removed, and much of the grade is now a hiking trail. Courtesy of David Parker.

Here at Slocan Junction, passengers could transfer to the eastbound or westbound trains of the CPR. They arrived here after taking the CPR sternwheeler from Arrowhead to Nakusp where rail connection was made to Roseberry on Slocan Lake. It was then by boat to Slocan City and by train to Slocan Junction. A long but certainly interesting journey!
Canadian Pacific Corporate Archives: A 17649.

In this photograph is the funeral train of Peter Veregin, arriving at Brilliant on October 29, 1924. The train carried 1,000 mourners to this headquarters of the Doukhobors and the final resting place of Peter "Lordly" Veregin.
Vancouver Public Library: photo 179.

77

When the CPR acquired the Columbia and Western Railway in 1898, it also acquired the smelter at Trail. The C & W and the CPR both had stations which were located on the bench above (adjacent to the Cominco plants), while the other station was downtown at the property where the Bay and Super Valu stores are now located. This station was replaced and relocated, and there are still two buildings with angled sides downtown to accommodate the tracks. The last passenger run into Trail was on August 1, 1949, and the tracks and station have long since been removed.
Cominco Archives and David Wilkie.

CPR Trail
Glenbow Museum.

The CPR station at Castlegar was built in 1907, replacing an earlier structure constructed in the same year but destroyed by fire. The style of architecture betrays its European origins with the shingled awning running the entire circumference of the building. The six indented dormers on the second storey are a design feature that is also evident in the Nelson station. An interesting historical association with this station is the fact that Peter Veregin, leader of the Doukhobors, was assassinated with eight others by an explosion on the CPR day coach en route from Nelson to Vancouver. The actual time and location of this deed was shortly after one o'clock in the morning on October 29, 1924, two miles west of Farron.

Canadian Pacific Corporate Archives: A 2200.

*Phoenix was the centre of the Granby Consolidated Mining, Smelting and Power Company. Tons of iron ore were shipped to the smelters at Greenwood. Erected as a model town, it boasted "handsome business blocks of frame and brick construction." It was named after the resurrectionist bird of the Nile, "who was supposed to set fire to the nest when old, and deliberately perish in the flames only to rise once more from its ashes with vigour and vitality." The Great Northern Railway also had a branch line here. With prices depressed, the CPR pulled out in 1933, and no sign of the town remains. Substantial ore deposits remain, so perhaps the Egyptian legend will be re-enacted here.
Canadian Pacific Corporate Archives: A 17732.*

Cont. from pg. 63

boomed with them. In 1901 the CPR extended its line to Procter, up the lake from Nelson. However, due to the heavy cost of construction, a line was not built from that point to Kootenay Landing until the 1920s. It was opened for service in January 1931. This area is now a mere vestige of its former self.

Railway-dependent coal mining is now centred at Sparwood, with the coal being taken up the Windermere subdivision to the mainline for its destination at Roberts Bank. Overseas-bound fruit and produce are no longer transported by rail; such cargo is carried by truck, and with the exception of a Great Northern line (now Burlington Northern) to Trail, Hill's branch lines are merely a memory.

One may still see a station in the Great Northern architectural style at Salmo. It is somewhat similar to the former Great Northern station at Princeton, B.C. The British Columbia Coast Steamship Service ceased operations when the *Moyie* made its last run in April of 1957. Its sister ship, the *Minto*, had made its last run April 23, 1954. For a short while, barge service was maintained to lakeshore communities such as Procter and Lardeau, but this too has gone. With the flooding of the Arrow Lakes for the Columbia Dam mega-project, history is now literally underwater. Passenger service ceased in 1964, and most stations have vanished. Application has been filed to abandon what is known as the Boundary subdivision, and it will not be long before the only sound one hears along this once-vital railway will be that of hikers. Nature is set to reclaim the land, just about one hundred years after the railway-building began.

Part Five: Revelstoke

The Rocky Mountain section of the CPR, lying between Laggan (now Lake Louise) and Revelstoke in British Columbia, covers a distance of 147 miles. More difficulties in construction were encountered here than on any other part of the line, including the section north of Lake Superior. Following the driving of the last spike at Craigellachie on November 7, 1885, considerable attention had to be devoted to upgrading the line. "Wood was used almost exclusively in the first construction of the division crossing the mountains. Timber was abundant, and in this way the road was opened for traffic many months before it would otherwise have been possible."[26]

Considerations taken into account when surveying the line were that it was to be 100 miles from the international boundary, yet as far south as possible to mitigate the heavy snows of the north. Yet another consideration was to keep the grade at 1 per cent. This provision was adhered to except in the case of the Kicking Horse Pass section between Hector and Field. Here, the grade was 4.4 per cent, but the Dominion government was assured that this situation was only temporary. The actual summit of the line is the location of the former station site at Stephen, and for this section of track, brakemen were at the platform of every car. An early observer suggested that it was "amusing to see them jump from the cars and run alongside to watch the workings of the brakes."[27]

Within the mountain ranges, it became necessary to construct wooden Howe truss bridges to cross and recross the rivers. These were temporary and were to be eventually replaced with steel structures. The extensive tunneling required was made difficult by the presence of loose moraine material and clay, and many tunnels built under these conditions collapsed. In order to facilitate a secure roadbed for the railway, solid masonry walls were constructed up from the river's edge. It is a tribute to the workmen involved that these walls stand to this day.

The Selkirks were the next major obstacle, and the problems here were not that of the grade or construction, but of the danger resulting from heavy snowfalls and avalanches. During the winter of 1898-99, the recorded snowfall was 43 feet 88 1/2 inches, according to measurements taken on the platform at Glacier House. The rotary snowplows of the CPR were able to deal with the fallen snow, but the problems lay in the avalanches, which contained all manner of material, including snapped trees of large proportions. These avalanches thundered down at tremendous speeds and swept up the other side of the valleys, often severely damaging the two railway lines.

The need for snowsheds became obvious, and during the first winter of operation, civil engineers noted the extreme areas. In the summer of 1886, thirty-five sheds were constructed, followed by an increase to fifty-three in the summer of 1887. To withstand the force of these avalanches, the sheds were constructed of the strongest materials available. "Cedar timbers, mostly 12 inches by 12 inches, formed the crib-work, but Douglas fir (Oregon pine) was employed in members subjected to severe transverse strains. The bents, usually spaced about five feet centres, were built up of 12-inch by 15-inch timbers, securely braced and drift-bolted together."[28] During the summer, temporary track bypassed many of the snowsheds, thus enabling the tourist to view the splendours.

Cont. on pg. 102

Kamloops has had four CPR railway stations. The first station, constructed in 1886, followed the architectural precepts of the first wave of stations such as Mission Junction. It was replaced in 1907, and the new depot was described as being in the "bungalow style of architecture." The beautiful station garden shows the importance the CPR attached to the cosmetic amenities of their buildings. However, in 1948 it was announced by George H. Baillie, Pacific region vice-president, that it was to be remodelled "as the first streamlined station on the main line west of Field." In the 1970s it was replaced by the existing station. The once-beautiful gardens became a parking lot!
BCARS: F-7445, F-5619, B-4475.

Kamloops' second station, 1907.

Kamloops' second station remodelled, 1948.

This was the second station at Sicamous, being built after fire destroyed the original depot in 1897. It was a resort station, although not on the grand scale of Field, Glacier and North Bend. The structure featured a central pavilion with polygonal turrets, and it had shingled walls with leaded glass windows. In 1910 an extension added twenty-five rooms, and patronage was steady until 1957 when passenger service to the Okanagan was eliminated and mainline service reduced. It was removed in July of 1964.
BCARS: A-959.

The station at Craigellachie was built in 1886. It was here where the last spike was driven on November 7, 1885. The station has long since gone, and a cairn now marks this historic site.
Canadian Pacific Corporate Archives: A 18338.

Revelstoke's first station was erected in 1886 and removed in 1908. The second station was one of the only large stations outside of the major cities. Contractors were Smith and Shelbourne, who constructed the station at a cost of $25,000. "The building was to be two floors above the ground, of mixed stone and brick, while from the contour of the place an extra storey of cut stone would be built below that." This view shows the Royal Visit in 1939. In 1978 this station was replaced by the present structure.
Kamloops and District Museum.

Williams Official British Columbia Directory of 1892 described Griffin Lake as follows: "A station on the main line of the CPR, 365 miles east of Vancouver and 17 miles from Revelstoke, has telegraph office, mails daily. Population 50."
Canadian Pacific Corporate Archives: A 18289.

The CPR resort station at Glacier was one of the most popular with tourists. Designed by Thomas Sorby and opened for service in 1887, it remained in operation until the summer of 1925 and was torn down in 1929. The heavy avalanches finally drove the CPR from Rogers Pass, and the "railway that had looped up from the valley and past the front door burrowed instead beneath a mountain."
Collection of the author.

Named after Major A.B. Rogers, the discoverer of the pass, the first station was built in 1886. Everyone in the picture except the girl in the light blouse was killed when a snow slide struck the station on January 9, 1899. She was a servant of the station agent's family. Collection of the author.

This station replaced the one destroyed in the avalanche of 1899. Rogers Pass was removed from the timetable in 1920.
Collection of the author.

The station at Beaver was the most northerly station on the transcontinental route. In this obviously-posed photograph, the station agent and his family appear amused by having their photograph taken. Kamloops and District Museum.

By 1904 the CPR had moved its divisional point from Donald to Golden. Houses of CPR employees in Donald were moved free of charge to Golden. The reason for the move was that the CPR planned to build a railway "from Golden on the mainline of the CPR to Fort Steele not far from the line of the Crow's Nest Pass Railway." This station was built in 1904 and was only recently closed. It is destined to become a museum. BCARS: E-1318.

This photo shows C.P. Rail Train Number One, Engs. VIA 1403, C.P. 8516 and VIA 1962 with an eleven-car consist entering Golden, B.C., Mile 35.0, Mountain subdivision at 6:10 p.m. 1-30-82. Photo by Dave Wilkie.

The first station at Field, B.C., was true to the architectural dictates of Cornelius Van Horne, who, when issuing instructions for the stations in the Rockies, said: "Lots of logs there. Cut them, peel them and build your stations." It reflected an appropriate air of cosiness and closeness to nature with the bellcast roof adding grace to the structure. It was removed in 1951.
BCARS: F-8377.

Field's second and present station is an example of the international style with the silhouette lettering, slab canopy and rectangular appearance. Field is slightly more elaborate than other examples of this style (Spence's Bridge and Cranbrook) due to its fieldstone base.
Michael Batten photo.

Designed by Thomas Sorby, Mt. Stephen House was the first of the resort stations to open. The fall of 1886 saw meals and accommodation being offered to train passengers. In 1901-1902 it was enlarged. Westbound trains stopped here for breakfast while eastbound trains stopped for supper. An 1897 CPR timetable described the location as "a favourite stopping place for tourists; excellent fly fishing for trout in a pretty lake nearby." BCARS: B-4054.

This station at Hector, B.C., was a rather basic structure and in keeping with the CPR policy of first getting the line opened for service and then refining the support facilities. It was soon replaced by a more dignified building. Hector was the start of the westbound 4.4 per cent downgrade which Van Horne had assured the government was only temporary. It was here that passengers disembarked for the CPR lodges at Lake Wapta and Lake O'Hara.
Canadian Pacific Corporate Archives: A 18236.

The station at Fort Steele was a familiar CPR design with living quarters in the second storey and the elongated freight shed. The long wooden platform allowed easy access to the station from both sides. Named after Major Steele of the N.W.M.P., this station has long since been removed, although a station exists here to serve a heritage steam railway.
BCARS: C-783.

Cont. from pg. 83

The Rocky Mountain division ended at Revelstoke where crews and engines were changed for the run to Port Moody, and later, Vancouver. "Thus the Rocky Mountain is crossed . . . which required the greatest patience and skill on the part of engineers entrusted with the task."[29]

Fully realizing the tourist potential of the Rockies and the whole CPR system in British Columbia, Van Horne, in characteristic mode, wasted no time in exploiting this potential. For as he said, "If we can't export the scenery, we'll import the tourists."[30] Comfort of passengers was of the prime concern to Van Horne, and while he did not overly concern himself with colonist car and second-class accommodation, he ensured that first-class passengers travelled in optimum comfort. Wide berths, self-contained toilet facilities and exquisitely appointed compartments were hallmarks of Van Horne. Sumptuous meals with a wide range of beverages were also part of the tourist package.

In addition, restaurant facilities were established at certain stations. The first to be constructed were the ones at North Bend (Fraser Canyon House), Glacier House at the foot of Rogers Pass and Mt Stephen House at Field near the foot of Kicking Horse Pass. In all cases, these resort hotels were designed by Thomas Sorby, a Victoria architect. They featured a three-storey centre flanked by two wings, one with two storeys, and the other with one.

A Swiss-chalet architectural style was used, the intent being to draw an association with the Alps of Switzerland. To further promote the Swiss "connection," Van Horne recruited Swiss mountain guides, notably Edward Feuz and Christian Hasler, who, in traditional Swiss mountain garb, guided climbers through the panoramic splendours of the Rockies. As a further inducement, free passage on freight trains and the use of velocipedes were provided to mountain access points.

In the last quarter of the nineteenth century, both in North America and Europe, the artist's hand was turning to nature at its most sublime. Interest in such scenic splendours, already popular in Europe, led to the formation of the Royal Canadian Academy of Artists in 1879 and then the founding of the National Gallery in 1882. It was no coincidence that this interest in capturing the grandeur and beauty of nature fused with Van Horne's desire for publicity of the scenic wonders along the railway. Thus began the railway school of art which in many ways was Canada's first attempt at national art, for here the scenic beauties of Canada were painted *a mari usque ad mare*. Van Horne appreciated the force and subtle persuasion of nature painting. He was himself an artist of note, as two of his paintings, "Moonlight on the St. Croix River" and "The Birch," testify.

Upon assumption of the vice-presidency of the CPR in 1884, Van Horne assumed the role of promotions manager. He authored *The New Highway to the Orient*, a pictorial publication extolling the scenery and features of the CPR. The Stony Creek Bridge in the Selkirks graced the front cover. The photographic firm of William Notman and Son of Montreal was recruited to photograph the progress of the railway.

Through the art world, Van Horne was aware of the Ontario Society of Artists, founded in June of 1872. Its first president, Lucius O'Brien, who was to become a famous painter for the CPR, executed splendid pieces of art such as "Gate of the Canyon" (1888) and "Cloud Capped Towers" (1886). John Fraser, a prominent artist, had had a falling out with O'Brien but was nonetheless commissioned to execute scenic portrayals of the Canadian landscape. His work, "The Rogers Pass," is a monument to the artists who have successfully portrayed the Canadian mosaic. Other artists of the Railway School were F.M. Bell-Smith, Thomas Mower Martin and George Horne Russell.

With the departure of Van Horne from the CPR, tourism promotion did not cease. Ski excursions, holidays at the resort stations and tours by rail throughout the nation continued to be prime holiday attractions until World War II. On many a station wall of those still in operation may be seen remnants of vacation-by-rail advertising. Attempts to revive the holiday splendour were made in the period after the war, but the travelling psyche of the Canadian public had transferred to the family automobile and airplane. By the 1920s the resort stations at Glacier and Field had closed down. On Vancouver Island, the CPR hotel at Strathcona on Shawnigan Lake had passed into private hands.

Bibliography

Original Sources

The Daily Colonist. (Victoria, B.C.) 1858-1980 (passim)
Nanaimo Free Press. (Nanaimo, B.C.) 1874 to date
Vancouver Sun. (Vancouver, B.C.) 1912 to date
The Victoria Daily Times. (Victoria, B.C.) 1884 to 1980 (passim)

Secondary Sources

Akrigg, Helen B. and G.P.V. Akrigg. *British Columbia Place Names*. Victoria, Sono Nis Press, 1986.

Alexander, Edwin P. *Down at the Depot*. New York, Clarkson N. Potter, Inc., 1970.

Baird, Ian. *A Historic Guide to the E&N Railway*. Victoria, Heritage Architectural Guides, 1985.

Begg, Alexander. *Canada and Its National Highway*. London, A paper read before the Society of Arts, March 23, 1886. (Canadian Institute for Historical Microreproductions No. 30352)

Canadian Pacific Railway — Western Lines — Private Instructions to Train Conductors. No.9. Winnipeg. April 16, 1928.

Droege, John A. *Passenger Terminals and Trains*. New York, McGraw-Hill Book Company, Inc., 1916.

Fleming, John, Hugh Honour and Nikolaus Pevsner. "Picturesque." *Penguin Dictionary of Architecture*. 1980, p.243.

General Publicity Department. *Canadian Pacific Facts and Figures*. Montreal, Gazette Printing Company, 1937.

Gibbon, John Murray. *Steel of Empire: The Romantic History of the Canadian Pacific, The Northwest Passage of Today*. Indianapolis/New York, Bobbs-Merrill, 1935.

Hart, E.G. *The Selling of Canada*. Banff, Altitude Publishing, 1983.

Innis, Harold A. *A History of the Canadian Pacific Railway*. Toronto, McClelland and Stewart, Ltd., 1923.

Kalman, Harold D. *The Railway Hotels — The Development of the Chateau Style in Canada.*, Victoria: University of Victoria, 1968.

Liddell, Ken. *I'll Take the Train*. Saskatoon, Western Producers Prairie Books, 1977.

Lotz, Jim. *Canadian Pacific*. London, Bison Books, 1985.

Maclachlan, Donald F. *The Esquimalt and Nanaimo Railway: The Dunsmuir Years: 1884-1905*. Victoria, British Columbia Railway Historical Association, 1986.

Martin, Edward J. *The Railway Stations of Western Canada*. Whiterock: Studio E Martin, 1980.

Province of British Columbia. Vancouver City, its progress and industries, with practical lists for capitalists and intending settlers. Vancouver, 1889. Canadian Institute for Historical Microreproductions No. 16310)

Roberts, Joseph. *The Origins of the Esquimalt and Nanaimo Railway: A Problem of British Columbia Politics*. Vancouver, University of British Columbia, 1937.

Sanford, Barrie. *McCulloch's Wonder: The Story of the Kettle Valley Railway*. Vancouver, Whitecap Books, 1977.

Shawnigan Lake Confederation Centennial Celebrations Committee of 1966-67. *Green Branches and Fallen Leaves*. Duncan, *Cowichan Leader.*, 1967 (1976).

Smith, Douglas M. "The Nakusp & Slocan Railway: Early Railway Days in the Kootenays," *Canadian Rail*, no. 410 (May-June 1989), pp. 81-88.

Turner, Robert D. *Vancouver Island Railroads*. San Marino, Golden West Books, 1973.

Vaughan, Walter. *The Life and Work of Sir William Van Horne*. New York City, The Century Co., 1920.

Vaux, William S. *The Canadian Pacific Railway from Laggan to Revelstoke* Philadelphia, 1900. (Canadian Institute for Historical Microreproductions No. 16325)

Wright, Arthur James. *The Winter Years in Cowichan*. Vancouver, University of British Columbia, 1967.

Notes

1. Robert D. Turner, *Vancouver Island Railroads* (San Marino: Golden West Books, 1973), p. 39.

2. See Joseph Roberts, *The Origins of the Esquimalt and Nanaimo Railway; a problem of British Columbia politics* (Vancouver: University of British Columbia, 1937).

3. Arthur James Wright, *The Winter Years in Cowichan* (Vancouver: University of British Columbia, 1967), p. 6.

4. Jim Lotz, *Canadian Pacific* (London, England: Bison Books, 1985), p. 14.

5. Ibid., p.49.

6. Alexander Begg, *Canada and its national highway* (London, England: A paper read before the Society of Arts, March 23, 1886), p.10.

7. Walter Vaughan, *The Life and Work of Sir William Van Horne* (New York City: The Century Co., 1920), p.368.

8. Lotz, *Canadian Pacific*, p.19.

9. John Fleming, Hugh Honour, Nikolaus Pevsner, *The Penguin Dictionary of Architecture* (London: Penguin Books, 1980) p. 243.

10. Ken Liddell, *I'll Take the Train* (Saskatoon: Western Producers Prairie Books, 1977), p.40.

11. Edwin P. Alexander, *Down at the Depot* (New York: Clarkson N. Potter, Inc., 1970), p.15.

12. John A. Droege, *Passenger Terminals and Trains* (New York: McGraw-Hill Book Company, Inc., 1916), p.253.

13. Ibid., p.267.

14. *General Publicity Department, Canadian Pacific Facts and Figures* (Montreal: Gazette Printing Company Limited, 1937), p.196.

15. "Ladysmith will have a new station," *The Daily Colonist*, May 20, 1944, p.5.

16. "Island Railway Notes," *Nanaimo Free Press*, July 18, 1885, p.4.

17. John Murray Gibbon, *Steel of Empire: The Romantic History of the Canadian Pacific, The Northwest Passage of Today* (Indianapolis/New York: Bobbs-Merrill, 1935), p.277.

18. *Province of British Columbia, Vancouver City, its progress and industries, with practical hints for capitalists and intending settlers* (Vancouver: 1889), p.8.

19. C.P.R. New Service to Nelson," *The Vancouver Sun,* July 28, 1916, p.5.

20. Barrie Sanford, *McCulloch's Wonder: The Story of the Kettle Valley Railway* (West Vancouver, B.C.: Whitecap Books, c1977), p.21.

21. Ibid., p.45.

22. "The Last Train from Penticton," *The Daily Colonist,* April 19, 1964, p.13, mag. sec.

23. Gibbon, p.339.

24. Douglas M. Smith, "The Nakusp-Slocan Railway: Early Railway Days in the Kootenays," *Canadian Rail,* No. 410 (May-June 1989).

25. *West of the Great Divide,* p.110.

26. Gibbon, *Steel of Empire,* p.344.

27. Ibid.

28. William S. Vaux, *The Canadian Pacific Railway from Laggan to Revelstoke, B.C.* (Philadelphia: 1900), p.75.

29. Ibid., p.68.

30. E.J. Hart, *The Selling of Canada,* (Banff: Altitude Publishing Ltd., 1983), p.7.

Index

Abbotsford, 19
Alberni, 31
Allan, Sir Hugh, 15
Arrowhead, 63
Bainbridge, 18
Bainbridge, R.A., 18
Banff, 16
Bauhaus, 18
Beaven, Robert, 14
Begg, Alexander, 15
Bell-Smith, F.M., 102
Billings, 19
Blackett, W.E., 23
Boat Harbour, 23
Brookmere, 51
Bryden, J., 14
Burrard Inlet, 32
Cameron Lake, 19
Carnarvon, Lord, 13
Castlegar, 18
Chemainus, 17, 20
Clement, L.M., 14
Coal Harbour, 32
Coalmount, 51
Cobble Hill, 23
Columbia and Kootenay Railway and Navigation Company, 48
combined freight and passenger station, 19
Coquihalla Pass, 62
Coquitlam, 18
Coryell, J.A., 48
Courtenay, 18, 31
Cowichan, 23
Craig's Crossing, 31
Craigellachie, 83
Creston, 17
Crocker, C.F., 14
Crocker, Charles, 14
Crown Zellerbach Logging, 23
Crowsnest Pass, 63
Dufferin, Lord, 13
Duncan, 17, 18, 20, 23
Dunsmuir Syndicate, 17
Dunsmuir, James, 14
Dunsmuir, Robert, 14, 23
Eholt, 48

Erikson, 17
Esquimalt, 19
Fernie, 18
Feuz, Edward, 102
Fiddick, Samuel, 31
Field, 19, 83, 102
flag station, 19
Fleming, Sir Sandford, 14
Fraser, John, 102
Fraser Canyon House, 102
Glacier, 19, 102
Glacier House, 83, 102
Goldstream, 20
Goldstream Hotel, 20
Grand Forks, 48
Great Central Lake, 31
Great Northern, 48
Hasler, Christian, 102
Hector, 83
Hedley, 51
Heinze, Augustus, 63
Heinze, Corbin, 63
Hill, J.J., 48
Hill, Louis J., 51, 63
Hitchcock, Henry-Russell, 18
Hope, 48, 51
Hope-Princeton highway, 18
Huntingdon, 32
Huntingdon, C.P., 14
Incola Hotel, 51
Janion Hotel, 14
Jayem, 31
Keremeos, 51
Kettle Valley Railway, 18, 48
Koksilah, 23
Kootenay Landing, 48, 82
Ladysmith, 20, 23, 31
Ladysmith Historical Railway Society, 23
Laggan, 15, 83
Lake Cowichan, 31
Lardeau, 82
Macdonald, John A., 13, 32
Mackenzie, Alexander, 13
MacLachan, Donald, 14
Maclure, Samuel, 20
Malahat, 18

107

Malahat station, 20
Martin, Thomas Mower, 102
Maxwell, Edward, 32
McCulloch, Andrew, 48
McKay, Michael, 51
Merritt, 51
Michel, 63
Midway, 48, 51
Minto, 82
Mission, 32, 46
Mission Junction, 46
Moberly, 18
Moyie, 82
Mt. Stephen House, 102
Nakusp, 63
Nanaimo, 14, 17, 20, 23
Nanaimo station, 31
Nanoose Bay, 31
Natal, 63
Nelson, 18, 48, 82
New Westminster, 32
North Bend, 19, 102
Northport, 63
Notman, William and Son, 102
O'Brien, Lucius, 102
Occidental Hotel, 31
Okanagan Falls, 51
Oliver, 62
Onderdonk, Andrew, 15
Onderdonk contract, 32
Osoyoos, 62
Othello, 51
Oyster Harbour, 23
Pacific Coast Collieries Railroad, 23
Pacific Scandal, 15
Page, Louis, 31
Parksville, 18
Parksville station, 31
Penticton, 51
Penticton station, 51
Phoenix, 48
Port Alberni, 18, 31
Port Moody, 32, 102
Princeton, 51, 82
Procter, 48, 82
Qualicum Beach, 18, 31
Quamichan Hotel, 31
Queen Victoria, 32
Quintette Tunnels, 51
Redgap, 31
Revelstoke, 19, 62, 83, 102

Robinson, Arthur L., 23
Robson, 48
Robson West, 63
Rosebury, 63
Rosser, Thomas A., 16
Rossland, 63
Russell, George Horne, 102
Russell's station, 20
Salmo, 82
Savona, 32
Shaughnesy, Thomas, 16, 48
Shawnigan, 23
Shawnigan Lake, 102
Shawnigan Lake Lumber Company, 23
Sicamous, S.S., 51
Slocan, 63
Slocan Junction, 63
Smithe, William, 13
snowsheds, 83
Solly Junction, 31
Somenos, 23
Sorby, Thomas, 102
Spence's Bridge, 62
Stanford, Leland, 14
Starks, 19
station gardens, 23
Stephen, 15, 83
Stephen, George, 16
Straits Lumber Company, 31
Stratford's Crossing, 23
Strathcona, 102
Strathcona Hotel, 20
Strathcona Lodge, 19
Three Forks, 63
Trail, 63
Trout Creek, 51
Tulameen River Valley, 62
Van Horne, Cornelius, 16, 32, 48, 62, 102
Vancouver, 18, 32
Vernon, 19
Victoria, 20
Victoria E&N station, 18
Walkem, George, 13
Wallace, A.E., 23
Warren, J.J., 51
Wellington, 14, 31
Wermer, 18
West Summerland station, 51
Westholme, 23
Wigwam, 62

Ian Baird, a native Victorian and professional librarian, has written extensively on railways and local history. He is employed as the Microforms Centre Supervisor in the McPherson Library, University of Victoria. Ian has a great interest in the world of secondhand books and operates a business, Empire Books, specializing in railroadiana, Canadian history and 19th Century British historical fiction. His first book, *A Heritage Guide to the E&N Railway*, focuses on railway stations of Vancouver Island, while the present work concentrates on C.P.R stations on the mainland. Ian plans a forthcoming book on grain elevators on the Canadian prairies.